The Last Conflict

The Durham Light Infantry
Borneo 1966

by

Mike Kelly
(ex-DLI and ex-Para 1965 -1973)

Designed by Sally Mundy

Printed and bound by Cromwell Press, Trowbridge, Wilts

This first edition published in 2004 by
Broadcast Books
84 Whiteladies Rd
Bristol
BS8 2QP

www.broadcastbooks.co.uk

This book is dedicated to the memory of
Alan Barella and Tommy Griffiths.

Alan Barella † **23.12.2003**

Tommy Griffiths † **26 02.1966**

Roll Call

2 Platoon Durham Light Infantry
Borneo February 1966

Commander JAG Arnot†
Lieutentant Kirk

Signals Fred Anwell

Medic. Bob Hall

Sergeant Thompson
Corporal P. Burns

Signals Pete Giddens

Signals Buck Williams

Corporal Bartlett†
Corporal D Creed

Lance Corporal Davies

L/Corporal S. Pugh†
Corporal Curly Wilson

Lance Corporal P Finn

Pte. Dennis Bailey
Pte. Bill Forman
Pte Garthwaite
Pte. Pete Hall
Pte Keith Hope
Pte. Kelly 26
Pte. Olly Olson
Pte. Andy Simpson†
Pte. Smaller
Pte. Keith Tweddle

Pte. Cooper
Pte. French
Pte. Tommy Griffiths†
Pte. Fred Hickman†
Pte. Ken Jackson
Pte. Oliver
Pte. Terry Reaper
Pte. Sloan
Pte Geordie Tuck
Pte John Valentine

† (deceased in bold)

In Memoria

The following soldiers from the DLI have died since the conflict:

Major J.A.G. Arnot MC
Major A.J.P. Grosch
Colonal McBain
Lt. Col. Maughan OBE
Lt. Eustace
R.S.M. Ford MID
C/Sgt. Sam Clark
C/Sgt. Alec Durham
Sgt. Major Ken Temple
Sgt. Jigger Brown
Sgt. Clark
Sgt. Day
Sgt. John Fishwick
Sgt. Fox
Sgt. J. Gahan
Sgt. Ben Halliwell
Sgt. Knowles
Sgt. McClung
Sgt. Bill McKeon
Sgt. Sherlock
Sgt. W. Staniland
Sgt. Joe Taylor
Sgt. John Trotter
Sgt. Wakefield
Sgt. Tommy Wardrobe
Cpl. D. Baron
Cpl. Tony Bartlett M.I.D.
Cpl. J. Cooper
Cpl. W. Dobbin
Cpl. Bob Griffiths
Cpl. Morrel
Cpl. Syd Quinn
Cpl. Allen Seed
Cpl. Tony Ward
Cpl. Curly Wilson
L/Cpl. J. Hubbucks
L/Cpl. Syd Pugh

Pte. Kenny Adams
Pte. Appleby
Pte. H. Barraclough
Pte. Alan Barella
Pte. D. Barrow
Pte. George Brandon
Pte. K. Cannon
Pte. E. Clarkson
Pte. Brian Constable
Pte. Harry Dunn
Pte. N. Flowers
Pte. Jackie. Gallon
Pte. F. Gaskell
Pte. Jim Gilchrist REME
Pte. Thomas Griffiths
Pte. Jacky Ham
Pte. F. Hickman
Pte. C. Higham
Pte. Kincaid
Pte. J. Lacy
Pte. K. Lynn
Pte George Mayo
Pte. R. Metcalfe
Pte. George Miller
Pte. Bill Mohan
Pte. J. Moore
Pte. Ralph Raine
Pte. R. Scales
Pte. Andy Simpson
Pte. Peter Slimmings
Pte. Willy Spalding
Pte. D. Stoker
Pte. T. Sudgen
Pte. Brian Wake
Pte. Ted Wheatley
Pte. J. Young

Contents

Uncle Billy, in his boxing days, who I have to thank for all that follows ...

Acknowledgments

Most grateful thanks are due to Alan Barella, for his constant encouragement, even in the last days of his unforgiving illness, as I was writing this book. He helped me with many memories and so wanted to be able to read the finished book, but did not live quite long enough to do so.

He was the smartest man in the company, a man's soldier. He said "Borneo days were the best days of my army life." Alan was like an older brother to me. He was a good listener, and whenever there was a job to be done, he would be there; if there was a problem he knew how to fix it. He showed me how to strip and clean the American Armalite, and showed me how to do everything the army way. Hard work was made light with Alan. He was a good, good friend, and I will miss him.

Grateful thanks are also due to the many friends and colleagues who have been so helpful with information and advice throughout the years it has taken to research and write this book. Thanks in particular to Frank Brannigan, Dougy Elliot, Allen Guy, Ken Milnes, Bob Noble, Terry Reaper and John (Tot) Taylor for their help in supplying illustrations, checking information, and in giving constant encouragement. Without them this book could not have been completed.

Picture Credits:

We acknowledge the generosity of the Imperial war Museum for their kind permission to reproduce the photographs on pp: 38, 40, 52, 54, 70, 78, 82, 88, 92, 96, 107, 109, 112, 128, 131. Many thanks also to Tom Collins of the Hartlepool Mail for the photographs on pages 12 and 20.

Major MacGregor-Oakford (MC), the officer commanding the Honour Guard, accompanying the queen on her inspection of the Durham Light Infantry Guard of Honour at the opening of the Tyne Tunnel in 1967.

Foreword

During 1963 and 1966 British troops were based in Borneo, fighting a secret jungle border war against Indonesia. It was a war which was kept so secret that not even parliament was informed by the Labour Defence Minister of the time, the Right Honourable Dennis Healey. Until the late eighties and early nineties, very little information about the war was made available. This was a war in which I took part, in what proved to be the final conflict of the DLI before peace was restored in Malaysia in August 1966. If these soldiers, who fought so bravely for their country have been forgotten, I at least will not forget them. I have set down here the story of our jungle patrols, leading up to the terrible day of 26th February 1966 which resulted in so many casualties, and the death of Pte. Griffiths - who was the last soldier to be killed in action whilst serving with the Durham Light Infantry. A week later Pte Miller also tragically died. Under enemy mortar fire we returned through the jungle from Indonesia into Sarawak carrying several wounded men together with the body of Pte. Griffiths; Pte. Bob Griffiths struggling with his grief as he walked beside the stretcher of his dead brother.

For gallantry during this day, Major Arnot was awarded the Military Cross and Lieutenant Kirk and Corporal Bartlett were mentioned in despatches. Ptes. Griffiths, Miller and Slimmings were all buried with full military honours in Singapore, where they lie to this day. Since then many of the young men who served in this campaign have died in their prime from cancer and incurable diseases. For what reason? Read the book and judge for yourself.

Mike Kelly (Ex-DLI & Ex-Para 1965 - 1973).

Medals won during the Borneo Conflict:

Victoria Cross Lance-Corporal Rambahadur Limbu
DCM: Lt./Col. 'Patch' Williams 2nd Battalion Parachute Regiment
DFC: Flying Officer Collinson (helicopter pilot)
Military Cross Major J.A.G. Arnot 1st Battalion DLI

Coaling on the beach near Hartlepool in the early 1960's

My brother Ernie still at it in his sixties today!

Chapter 1

Home in Hartlepool / The Steelworks / Harry Brewer & Boxing / Our Ernie / Coaling on the Beach / The Electrician and the punch-up / The Recruitment Office / Copthorne Barracks

I lived in Bellevue, as it was known in those days, the roughest part of Hartlepool in County Durham. Ours was a 'two-up & two down' terraced house, with the toilet in the back yard and no bathroom - apart from a Belfast sink in the kitchen, which had cold running water. In my mind's eye, I can remember a great cast-iron fire range which was constantly hot, and had a cast-iron kettle steaming on the hob.

Our house had few modern conveniences beyond a television whose antenna stuck out into the front garden. My mother, bless her soul, kept the house tidy - despite my three brothers and a sister who were still at home and weren't the tidiest of people.

I attended Oxford Street Junior School and Elwick Road Secondary Modern School which I left in 1963 to begin working for a metal fabricator earning £2/6/- a week (£2.30 in today's money). I worked there for a year, then started at the steel works for an extra £3 a week on shift work. By early February 1965, I was still working in the North Works of the South Durham Steel & Iron Company in Hartlepool Rolling Mills.

I had the job of marking the gauge of the hot steel plates coming out of the rollers, together with a man named Harry Brewer (whose boxing name was Pat Gaumont). He had held the British Empire Championship belt alongside Teddy Gardner - another great champion during the fifties and who had also fought a European Championship fight.

As I went on my shift, I would try to avoid Harry because he would try to use me as a sparring partner and when he hit me, it hurt. He said that it was the only way I was going to learn, if ever I wanted to become a boxer. He urged me to join the Boys' Welfare Club where they would train me to box. He told me what great boxers my father and grandfather had been and that I would be letting them down if I didn't take up the Noble Art, and added that he would be backing me all the way! So I joined the club and after a couple of months they told me how well I was doing. I, however, I wasn't at all sure that I wanted to spend the rest of my life fighting. I wanted a career and if the only way I could achieve this was by joining the army, then that is what I wanted to do. My only problem was how I was to tell Harry.

One of my favourite haunts was the Steel Works Club. On the ground floor was a bar where the working man had exclusive rights - no women were allowed. Here, a great deal of bragging was done and you could hear the local lads discussing the local girls in quiet tones. The older workers' talk was mainly about work and the new pipe mill that was opening at Port Clarence. There were three snooker tables on the top floor, and behind the club was a small gymnasium where my uncle Billy Kelly was in charge of the boxing.

All Harry wanted was another North-East champion and I did not like to let him down. I finally got the bottle to tell him when we were on the night shift and I was going into No1.rolling mill. Harry was there alone at the finishing rolls, gauging the hot plates with a set of callipers, and doing my work as well as his own. He was not very pleased. I was late and I had to suffer the 'silent treatment' for the first hour. In between the ingots coming out of the furnace, he offered me one of his sandwiches. He was good like that, but I still had to keep my eye on him - just in case he tried to dig me in the ribs, as he often did! I thought that this would be a good time to tell him because the mill was 'on stop' with a breakdown caused by an ingot getting jammed in the push furnace as the overhead crane was coming down the mill, and one of the finishing rolls had broken clean in half. This was serious and all the managers were coming down to investigate.

Harry started to tell me that this was the very crane my uncle Danny had fallen from twelve months previously when he was doing some electrical maintenance work. He had been killed outright. I remember it well. The very spot where he had landed was within a few feet of where I was working. It took a long time for my father to get over his death as he himself was working in the sheet mill at the time of the accident. After that day my father gave up working in the steelworks.

I finally got around to telling Harry that I didn't want to take up boxing, though I didn't want to hurt his feelings. I told him I wanted to go into the Parachute Regiment. He put his hand on my shoulder - for a minute I thought he was going to punch me - and he said, "If you really want to go into the army, it would do you more good than boxing and I would still be just as proud!"

I explained to Harry that my school friend for the last ten years, Mick Witham, had just passed his Para course and gone into the 7th Royal Horse Artillery (RHA) in the 16th Parachute Brigade (known as '7 Para'). Hearing this, Harry didn't mind at all.

At about this time, the manager of No.1 Mill sacked Harry's brother Bertie who had been in charge of the 'rolls' at the time of this very rare accident. Many thousands of pounds worth of damage had been caused. The whole workforce of the North East Steel Industry decided to walk out on strike to get Bertie reinstated, and this is how we spent the next two days until it was 'sorted' and the mill was back to normal.

It also happened that we were having some trouble at home. Two of my brothers, Martin and Danny, had been sent to an Approved School for stealing and as I was still only seventeen, I was not about to let this happen to me. The 'School Board Man' (Truancy Officer) would call every day about my eldest brother Ernie, but they would never find him: he would be on the beach pulling coal off.

At that time each of the coastal pits, Blackhall, Horden and Easington, had an aerial bucket system that carried the coal waste on wire ropes overland to the beach where it would all be tipped into the sea. It was a convenient waste disposal system, which resulted in black, polluted beaches from Hartlepool to Seaham. This waste - mainly slate and unsaleable coal muck - was tossed back and forth by the action of the waves and the coal nuggets amongst it, being lighter than the rest of the muck were thrown back up on the beach, where it could conveniently be gathered and shovelled into lorries then hauled off to be sold later. Sometimes a hundred tons could be washed up.

Ernie collected the coal with a barrow that he had made out of a box. It had a couple of shafts on either side and was harnessed with a piece of rope that went round his shoulders to assist in the pulling up the steep cliff path from the beach.If Ernie was coming off the beach in the early hours, he would wake half of Belle Vue from their sleep as he came down Oxford Street with the rattle of the great iron wheels he had fixed on his barrow. His black and white mongrel dog would have its front paws up on the back of the barrow trying to push as Ernie pulled between the shafts. Next morning, he would 'bag' the coal and sell it around Hartlepool at two bob a bag. Helping to support our family meant that his school days were few - though without his help we would have starved.

Ernie would do anything to make a bit of money. If there was no coal on the beach, he would use his horse and four-wheel cart to go round the back streets of Hartlepool shouting "Rag an' Bone!" He would swap goldfish for old rags or scrap for as long as he was able to weigh it in every day at Stan Pout & Foster's Scrap Dealers in the long back street. He was so good at it that he would re-load his cart three times a day. When he reached the age of seventeen, Ernest made his barrow redundant and bought himself an ex-army lorry, last used during World War II. The American troops had brought them over to the UK and they were sold on by auction when they were no longer required.

When I was finishing my shift at the Rolling Mill I would often go and help him when he was on the beach, which would be in all weathers - probably just to avoid going home. We would sometimes be there night and day, whatever the weather; very often lashed by gale-force, North East winds and snow blizzards; waiting for the tide to turn. When I think back on it, at least we had been able to light a fire on the beach to warm ourselves now and then and we would be 'grafting' so hard with the shovels, that we didn't really feel the cold so much. So, you could say that I was inured to this weather and even when I was working at the steelworks, I would look forward to going over the steelworks' bridge and straight down to the beach where I could meet up with my brother for a hard night's graft.

I would normally arrive on the beach about 11.30 at night via the short walk over the old steelworks bridge. This bridge was constructed of wood, and between every piece of wood there was an inch gap for heat expansion where you could see the railway track below. As the train passed, the steam would rise up through the Bridge slats and totally blind you for a few minutes until it was gone. It was a bit frightening.

There was one night I would not forget. My brother had been on the beach for about three tides working on the same patch of coal. If the tide washed the coal up at a certain place, you could count on its being in the same place for the two or three days following. This night when I arrived, the rain was lashing into my face and I had to lean into the wind to stop myself being blown off my feet. I could see the lights of his old ex-army lorry at the low water mark. As I approached, I could hear shouting and when I drew nearer, I was surprised to see that the lorry was bogged down to its axles in the sand and that Ernie was frantically trying to get it out. With the tide coming in fast, the tops of the wheels were soon covered and we could see its headlights still shining through the waves as they pounded the side of the cab of the lorry. This went on for about half an hour and all the other sea-coal traders came to help.

That was how it was - if someone got into trouble, there was always help at hand, only this time it was useless. Ernie was swimming towards the shore as the tide covered the lorry, still with its lights flashing, as each wave crashed over it. The only thing to do was to wait until the tide went out again and then hire a ten-ton Commer-winch lorry (another 'Army Redundancy') and our lorry would be recovered and taken back to a yard where the engine would be cleaned out and the oil changed. A new set of points and it would be back on the beach for the next tide. This was my elder brother. He had worked all his life - even through his 'School Days' that he never attended. He was quite illiterate, but at making a shilling he was excellent.

At this time we all slept in one room, about twelve feet square with two beds (a single bed and a 'double'). If one of us slept in the wrong place we would fight like dog and cat - even at three o'clock in the morning, when my father would walk in and sort the lot of us out. He had started working in the 'Prop Field'. This was one of several vast storage yards for the stacks of timber - railway 'property' - that had been unloaded onto rail trucks from the boats docking at Hartlepool. He had been hod-carrying, and had to get up for work the next morning.

When it was Friday my mother would not see any of his wage packet. That day he would go straight into the pub, where he would stay until he got thrown out and came home pissed with his mates singing, about midnight. Then he would turn nasty and take it out on my mother. It was always about religion. He was a Catholic and my mother was Protestant - if this was just an excuse for a row we will never know. On this particular night we went to bed and listened to the row going on downstairs, which was getting more and more violent, and lasted well into the morning.

When we got up, my mother sported a black-eye and bruising and we couldn't do a thing about it, because my father would kill us if we tried. I learned later from Ernie that my mother had got her own back and split my father's head with a poker later that day, and the wound needed eighteen stitches!

Yet when my mother fell ill with cancer a few years later my father collected her from the hospital and nursed her during those final months with great devotion and gentleness. She died in my arms in the front room of our house.

I could always handle myself, but I was no match for my father. That is why I had to join the army to get some sort of different life to this. I suppose at the time I felt a bit of a coward for leaving her to this fate, but I knew that the only real solution was for me to join the army, and this decision was gradually arrived at after an interesting episode.

Early in 1965, on a very rare night, I visited the Blacksmith Arms in Stranton (the 'White House'), directly opposite the Gaumont cinema and adjacent to another pub, the Seven Stars. I was only seventeen and under age, but nobody seemed to notice.

This was going to be a night I would never forget. I was having a drink in the bar. I was accepted and was having a conversation with two or three other men and having a really good time. I noticed that one of the men who was about six feet tall, had some sort of a strap on one of his hands,

I realized that he was disabled. He told me that he was an electrical engineer in the steelworks and that he knew my father and late uncle Danny who was killed there. He said that he used to work on the same shift as him.

The men left the pub before I did and I followed a bit later with a few younger mates - all working at No.1 Mill - Mick Cameron and a Michael Dovner, whose nickname was 'Stud'. We were going to the local dance hall, the Queen's Rink. On the way we passed the Art Gallery and Museum which was surrounded by iron railings. There was some sort of commotion going on in the grounds. I looked over and saw these four men kicking hell out of a poor man who was lying on the ground. I looked again and realised that it was the electrician we had just been talking to earlier in the pub. I said to my three mates, "Come on lads - he works in No.1 Mill! We've got to help him!"

They told me to fuck off and added that if I wanted to help him I was on my own. So I jumped over the railings and grabbed the first one I came to by the jacket. I pulled it over his head and kicked the shit out of him. Then I grabbed the next one, who was nearest me and put him on the deck too. When the other two realised what was going on they ran away. It was all over and had lasted about thirty seconds. The electrician was in a right mess so I helped him up to his feet. I asked him if he wanted me to help him home but he said he could manage on his own, so I left him and set off down the road towards the dance hall. After I had cleaned myself up, I met my so-called 'mates' again. Despite what had happened, we still had a good time.

While at the dance I saw two lads in army uniform and I realised that I knew them. - Brian Constable and Charlie Bassett. We had been to school together and been good mates. They told me that they had joined the army and were having a great time. It was the best thing they had ever done, they said. Every day I would hear that some more of my mates were joining the army and from then on I spent a few nights in the pub on my own thinking what I was going to do with my life.

A week later I went into the Blacksmith's Arms again, and I think I had only about two bob (10p) in my pocket. A pint of Strongarm was one shilling and sixpence (7.5p). It was 9.30pm and I was hoping that my elder brother Ernie would walk in and buy me a pint - otherwise I would be going home early - when this big fella walked in with his mates and stood at the bar. It was the electrician. After about ten minutes, he looked across at me in amazement and exclaimed, "You are the one from last week!" I said, "Yes, I am." He shook my hand and introduced me to all his mates. He had already told them about what had happened the week before and said, "Only a Kelly would do what you did that night! I know your dad and your grandfather and all your family."

Well, I didn't have to put my hand in my pocket again whilst I was in their company. He was very interested in what I intended to do with my life when I told him that I intended joining the Parachute Regiment, if I could get accepted. He told me that I couldn't do a better thing and that if he were still a youngster he would do the very same thing. He advised me to get out while I had the chance, because if they nationalised the Steel Industry, the North Works would certainly be closed down - and he was a man to know, because he was an important man in the Boiler Makers Union. If I ever needed anything, I was to come and see him and he would give me anything I wanted.

It was confirmed shortly after that they were about to nationalise the Steel Industry and that there would be a lot of redundancies - over two thousand men would lose their jobs. It would be an economic disaster for Hartlepool. That is when I finally decided to get some information at the Recruitment Office on York Road, and there I met Sergeant Jim Murray of the Durham Light Infantry. I told him that I would like to enlist in the Parachute Regiment, but I had to go back several times to make the same request because each time he tried to persuade me to join the DLI, which he insisted was the next best thing to the Paras. He suggested that I do a couple of years with the Infantry and then to put in for a Para course called 'P' Company. I would find it a lot easier than jumping straight into the deep end. I thought that this made a lot of sense and decided to take his advice. There was, however, another hurdle to cross. I would have to get my parents' signed permission on the Consent Form, because I was only seventeen years old.

I would have to think this through. Close to the Recruitment Office - a bit handy I thought - was a small coffee bar called The Yorkshire Lass, where all the local Teddy Boys used to hang out. It had a Wurlitzer blasting out rock-an'-roll music and it was a real delight to sit in there taking in the clothes and the shoes, but most of all the girls with their bright skirts and snug-fitting tops. What an atmosphere! There was the constant clanging of the flipper machine bells and couples jiving in the space in the centre of the floor. My own suit was a grey one with a black velvet collar and then there were the crepe shoes together with drainpipe trousers - How on earth I got into them I still can't figure out!

It was all much easier than I had feared. After talking to my mother she said that if that was what I wanted to do, she had no objections. My father took no convincing. He said it would do me a lot of good. Really, I was quite shocked because I never thought that he would agree so easily. In fact, I had caught him at the right moment. He had just come in from the pub with his mates and a crate of Newcastle Brown Ale. I knew that once he had said something in front of his mates he wouldn't go back on it, also it would give him something to brag about in the pub if he had a son in the army.

So off I went to the Recruiting Office and from there they sent me to another Recruiting Office in Middlesborough to receive the 'Queens Shilling' and sign on in Her Majesty's Armed Forces. I was issued with a travel warrant for Copthorne Barracks, Shrewsbury, Shropshire.

Dressed in my new grey velvet collar suit and winkle-picker shoes, I made my way by train to Shrewsbury station and walked into the car park area. I noticed about fifteen lads waiting to board the Bedford truck that was our transport to the barracks. When we arrived, we had a roll-call and were then escorted to the Quartermaster's Stores and reported to the CQMS (Company Quartermaster Sergeant) to draw our uniforms and other kit. Next thing, we were marched to the barber shop where we were shorn like sheep. After we were allocated to our sleeping quarters we walked into massive buildings with sparkling shiny floors. To the left and right were offices controlled by the non-commissioned officers (NCO's) and the platoon commander had one of these rooms as his personal office for the administration of the new recruits.

My allocation was on the first floor and when I entered the billet I found a large room with shining parquet flooring. Old cast-iron radiators hung on the wall, and under each of the windows there was a single steel bed - eight in all down one side and the same number down the other side. Each bed had a steel locker at its foot. A bedside cabinet in 'light oak effect' was also provided. The only decoration allowed was a picture of Her Majesty Queen Elizabeth II, which hung on the far wall. The subdued, bland, pale blue walls gave a cool feeling. This was to be our home for the next fifteen weeks.

The lads were from different parts of the country, all expecting to go to their own County Regiments. We had to be on parade at 08.00hrs and next morning we were marched onto the parade ground with our army issue denims and khaki shirts itching like hell till we got used to them. We looked a right shower of shite and were constantly screamed at to get in step. A Major Lane told us that we had a tough 15 weeks ahead of us!

Our home for the next 105 days was to be the Inkerman Block - other blocks were also named after famous battle honours such as Anzio and Minden.

The yard at Hartlepool Steel Works taken from the bridge, in the 1960's

Chapter 2

Initial Training / Wrekin Hill / Accident / 'Double March' / Trouble in the Barrack Room / In the Guard Room / 'Dishonourable Discharge' / The 'Cookie'/ Punishment Regime / My Friend the Bin / My Grandad / The DLI

It had all started - the 'bull' - which was the endless polishing, the drill, the weapons training and, of course, the discipline! After about the third week it was 'Assessment Week' and six of our number were discharged. Three were 'back-squadded' to start training again and that left 23 of us to start the fourth week. The NCO's in charge of our training were Corporal Nelson ('Nellie') Basset, Corporal Wood, Corporal Ben Halliwell and Sergeant Dewar, the platoon sergeant. Sergeant Dewar was in charge of doing inspections on your kit. If it wasn't up to standard, it would be pulled out of your locker and thrown all over the floor and this procedure would be repeated 'until we got it right'!

At about this time, the staff realised we had two 'Potential Officers' amongst our number. These were Pte Geoffrey Gamlin (later to become Padre Gamlin) and Pte Richard May (later to become Lieutenant May) who eventually came to the DLI. Both were well educated and were good lads. Richard and I were quite good mates and we would go down to Shrewsbury Town Centre on Friday and Saturday nights. The cider and I didn't get on too well together but we did have some good times - of course we would regret it all on Monday morning when we were back in training, slightly hung-over.

On Monday morning, we were back on parade and being taught how to dress so that we looked half-decent in the baggy denims and shirts that were two sizes too big for us. The only thing we had to get right now were the brasses on our belts and the gaiters that went round our ankles. To have "GET IT RIGHT!" screamed at us every morning, with the sergeant's nose about two inches from my own, day in and day out, wasn't my idea of fun.

It was time for us to be introduced to the live firing range known as Wrekin Hill just outside Shrewsbury. We arrived in four tonners (Bedford lorries) with full battle dress. The first thing that happened was that Corporal Nellie Basset started screaming that we should "Get fell in!" and prepare to run up this huge hill without stopping. We all thought that he was "Fucking joking" but, knowing Nellie, we had a sinking feeling that this wasn't so.

We started 'at the double' and went up for a steep 500 feet - and I mean STRAIGHT UP. When we all got to the top without stopping, we expected a rest, but this was not to be. As we approached the top, there was Nellie waiting for us to send us right back down again as fast as our legs would carry us, falling over each other and with his big mouth screaming alongside us. When we arrived at the bottom, we were each issued with twenty 7.62 live rounds to fill a magazine, load the weapon and fire into the butts at 'figure eleven' targets. These targets were shaped like a full-sized German soldier coming towards you, which we were expected to hit with every round. We started firing. Almost immediately. I heard a huge bang and felt splinters hitting me. The soldier next to me was screaming as the barrel of his SLR (self-loading rifle) had exploded into about seven different pieces. As they rushed him off to hospital, we realised what must have happened on our little run up the hill. He had fallen over and stuck the muzzle of his weapon into the ground, completely obstructing the barrel with mud. Well, that was another lesson learnt.

It was getting late. We had fired about a hundred rounds each and had a really exciting day out. We started to clean our weapons in the afternoon with the sun shining when, to our amazement, the four tonners started pulling away down the road till they were out of sight. We were gutted. I heard one of the lads say they were having a laugh, but they weren't. We heard "On your feet lads!" Yes, we were marching back and Nellie called for 'Double March' so that we would be in time for the cookhouse and a late meal. By the time we had covered fifteen miles, we had reached the end of the A5 into Shrewsbury and were spread out over half a mile. We were regrouped and then expected to march in an orderly fashion, with Nellie screaming as usual.

By the time we got to the camp gates, anybody would think we had just come out of the 'boozer' as some of the lads could not even walk because of blistered feet. Once in the barrack room, removing our boots was a blessed relief. We expected that almost half the platoon would be at the Medical Centre with sore feet and backs.

This was when trouble started in the platoon. Some money had gone missing out of my locker. I had seen someone by my bed space and when I got there, I missed the money. I turned and saw a big dark-skinned man - I forget his name - staring at me. I said, "What the fuck are you looking at ?" and he came at me almost immediately with a bayonet. My first thought was, was he trying to kill me? I went for him. I didn't have much choice as he was coming for me like a fucking lunatic. I grabbed his arm but not before the point of the bayonet went into my wrist. There was blood everywhere. The lads managed to part us and the soldier was thrown out of the army two days later. I wished it had never happened.

I had to go to the Medical Centre and the MO (Doctor) on duty requested that the orderly, a Sergeant Croucher who looked a right bastard, put six stitches in the wound. I told myself that, God help me, I would feel every one of them as he put them in. He was whistling all the time and I could not even remember his giving me an injection, he was so quick and mean.

I was getting on with my training quite well but on the sixth week of my course I had another 'set to'. It all happened because I cannot stand seeing a big man throw his weight around on young squaddies. I was in bed after having had a few pints in the NAAFI, when I heard shouting. I flew out of bed only to find them brawling in the middle of the floor, so I grabbed the biggest and hit him so hard that he went backwards five paces with the force of the punch. As he ran, another man started 'mouthing' at me, so I grabbed him too and hit him so hard that he went backwards over a locker and he ran…crawled…straight to the guard room, unknown to me.

I went back to bed and about 04.00 we were awoken by the White Belts (Regimental Police) who placed me under arrest. They ordered me to get dressed and then took me to the guard room 'at the double' (double-pace) and on the way told me that the second man I had hit was in hospital with a rupture gained after hitting the locker. The White Belts thought that I had kicked him where it hurts the most. Fortunately for me this was not true.

When I got to the guard room, they formally charged me with 'Grievous Bodily Harm' and I was put in the cells until next morning when I was put straight in front of the Commanding Officer, a Lieutenant Colonel Salisbury-Trelawney. I was marched into his office 'at the double' and the charges were read out aloud. I knew I was in real trouble. The summary trial and my explanation took about ten minutes. He had his mind made up and he passed sentence. He gave me 28 days in the guardroom and a dishonourable discharge. I was totally devastated at this decision. I did not get a chance to say anything and was marched out to begin my sentence.

From 'day one' it was punishment. I went for my meals 'at the double' (double-time running). After running to the cookhouse on a daily basis, the 'cookie'- a small weedy, weasel that, after feeding me extra food on top of my daily ration tried to get into my confidence - although, as a prisoner, I wasn't allowed to speak to anyone. It became apparent what he was after later on.

I will try to give an indication of what life was during a stay in the army punishment block. Up at 06.00 hours, after a wash and a regulation shave (You would have to ask for a razorblade and return it afterwards immediately afterwards!). There was the first kit-inspection of the day.

My bed had to be stripped down and the blanket laid on it so tightly that it would not move if a two-bob piece (10p) was dropped on it. Next came the 'bed-pack' - the sheets and blankets fitted together in a certain way so that each item would be shown individually, just in case I had secreted away any item to assist in escape. My other items of highly polished kit were also to be laid out in a particular way - the brasses, the webbing belt, the highly-polished boots, No.1 cap with brim glistening. After setting up the bed for inspection, I would have to take my mess tins over to the back door of the cookhouse to collect my breakfast and also breakfast for the two other inmates who were being shipped out to Colchester Glasshouse (the main army prison for any offence requiring over 56 days of detention.) After breakfast, I would have to clean my own mess tins together with knife, fork and spoon, ready for kit-inspection.

Once I had got the bed ready, I would then turn my attention to the general cleanliness of the guard room. I would have to polish the floor until you could see your face in the reflection. After the first kit-inspection of the day, it would be 'Exercise Period' - not like civilian prisoners milling around without purpose, but constant hard drill. This drill wasn't parade ground drill, but guard room drill with the Provost Sergeant Monty Banks screaming orders - a bit like circuit training, only a lot harder and without rest periods. That took care of the mornings.

At lunch time, I would be 'doubled' over to the cook house to get lunch for myself and the other two. Lunch was also a hurried affair and you were only given a certain amount of time to eat it and clean up after yourself. If you went outside this time allowance, more time would be added to your sentence. After the 'leisurely' lunch break, you were allowed the luxury of a cigarette - a luxury that followed every meal break. We would then get our kit ready for our next inspection, which involved polishing brasses and 'bulling' our boots until the toes were like polished black glass.

By the time this work was finished, it would be around 14.00 hours and it was back to the parade ground. Constant hard exercise was how the real hard men of the British army were created. Hard muscles were turned into blocks of hardened steel. You would do two or three circuits of the parade ground then drop to the ground and do fifty press-ups. By around 15.00hrs, the hard exercise would have been done and then it would be back to the 'bull', polishing and cleaning, and finally we could have a hot shower.

The evening meal was at 17.00hrs and the mess tins had to be gathered for collecting the food before then. By 17.30hrs our kit had to be got ready for inspection again and this brought us up to 18.00hrs. The guard would be changed at 19.00hrs with an inspection by the Orderly Officer and after the guard's inspection it was our turn. Depending on the mood of the Watch Commander, we might get a cup of tea just before bedtime at around 20.30hrs. This unvarying timetable was followed every single day when I was in the guard room.

On 'Day Two', the Provost Sergeant, Sergeant Banks, appeared to take an instant dislike to me because of what I had done -or this was my impression at the time.

I subsequently found out that it was his job to make my life as unpleasant as possible. He carried a dustbin into the guard room and I heard my name called in a loud voice. I 'doubled' from my cell and stood to attention in the front part of the guard room where it dawned on me that the dustbin was meant for me. It was to become my best friend. Sergeant Banks continued roaring just as if I wasn't present and he gave the world to understand that this dustbin was meant for Kelly to polish and he added, "…By the time he gets out of here, it will be GLEAMING!". There was no doubt but that he meant it. I polished that bin for two hours a day - though I had other polishing duties, which included the large brass fire alarm bell suspended from a bracket hanging outside the guard room whilst Lance Corporal Crisp stood over me. He was a man of very dubious parentage and he is one man I will never forget!

One night, I was relaxing in my cell - it being night time you could feel totally at ease (I am, of course, not being quite truthful - there was a one inch diameter spy hole at the top of the steel door so that the guard could look through and check that you were not trying to commit suicide!) - but this night the flap opened and cigarettes and matches came through, so I knew I had someone out there who was on my side. I found out later that it was Kilty and Scottie. They well knew what had happened during that fateful night because they were there, but of course, the British army didn't feel the need for witnesses! Still, that's another story.

When I was about half-way through my sentence, I asked the Duty Officer in charge, a Lieutenant Drury, if I could see the Company Commander Major Lane and permission was granted. That same day I went before him and asked him if he would request the colonel to reconsider his verdict. He said that he would put my case forward.

In the meanwhile, I was to remain in the 'Nick' (guard room) where I was nearly coming to the end of my sentence. Finally, I was informed that the C/O (commanding Officer), had decided to see me and I was marched in again. This time, however, I was given the opportunity to explain my side of the story.

As I stood in front of him, he said, "Can you give me one good reason why I should keep you in the army ?" I replied, "Well sir, my father was in the DLI and the Airborne Forces as was my grandfather in both World Wars. My ambition was to go into the DLI then, after a couple of years, do a P Company' Course (a very tough 15 week Para course) and after passing, to transfer to the Parachute Regiment. I do regret what I have done and probably will continue to regret it for the rest of my army career, if I am allowed to continue."

The C/O could see that I was upset (I was nearly crying).I thought that the shame of returning to Hartlepool with a 'Dishonourable Discharge' would be too much to bear. The shame of meeting my father. My grandfather had been a great man who, during his career, had been decorated by his regiment the DLI. He had also gained the Africa Star, the Burma Star and others too numerous to mention. More than that, he was my hero. He had fought 'Philadelphia Jack O'Brien' for the Light Welterweight Championship of the World in 1923 - unfortunately he had come second. In later years, he suffered from the injuries he had gained during the two World Wars. He suffered from 'wandering shrapnel' and it caused gangrene in both legs and he had to have them amputated above the knees. Even in a wheel chair he was a formidable man…the very thought of the disgust this man would hurl at me I could not bear to dwell on.

"I will give you this chance…If you come before me again, for any reason, there will be no more chances!" the C/O said to me. He added as I left, "If you want to fight, you are going to the right regiment. I am sending you to the regiment of your choice - the 1st Battalion, the Durham Light Infantry, if you pass all the rest of your training.

I served the final week of my sentence, but I didn't care what they threw at me. One more week of running, press-ups and screaming were not going to beat me. I was more determined than ever to make the most of this chance - which you don't usually get in the British army. I was not going to be beaten in the last few days. As I still had 'my friend the dustbin' that I had really looked after during the last month, I just hoped that the next prisoner would look after it as well as I had. The last day finally came and I was released.

Chapter 3

'Back-Squadded'/ Minden Platoon / Meeting 'Cookie' again / The Gas Chamber / 'Stand by your Beds!'/ The Brecon Beacons / Thunder Flashes in the Night / Forced March / Training Completed

The platoon that I was to join was named Minden and was under a Sgt Hassle who was SCLI (Somerset & Cornwall Light Infantry). I also remember well a Corporal Ian Morrell, a tall man of over six feet who was to become my best friend in the later part of my service career. We had a lot in common. He transferred to the SAS at the same time that I went to the Parachute Regiment.Unfortunately, he got posted to Northern Ireland and was killed. I lost a great friend.

It felt strange to be amongst the lads once more. No one spoke to me for a couple of hours, because they all knew that I had just come out of the 'Nick', so I took things as they came and I got on quite well after that. I started my training with this platoon on 'Week 3' - I had been 'back- squadded' a month. This is where I met Jack O'Connor and Nobby Martin who were experienced soldiers, having done their National Service with the 2nd Battalion the Parachute Regiment and the Royal Artillery respectively. Jack turned out to be a great mate and taught me everything I should know about the army - even that wearing a pair of nylon socks underneath our army issue would prevent us getting blisters. It worked!

He told me that when he finished his National Service, he just couldn't settle or adjust to civvy street, so he re-enlisted. Whilst I was under Jack's supervision, I didn't get 'confined to camp' very often. Everything was going right and we had more nights out. This made me more determined to transfer to the 16th Parachute Brigade.

I had been 'conned' by the Cook house 'cookie'. He had told me that he was a corporal in the Catering Corps and borrowed money from me. This went on for a couple of weeks until I heard that he was borrowing money from every recruit on the camp, and I got wise and found out that he was really a civilian cook!

One night, Jack O'Connor and myself went down to Shrewsbury Centre for a drink and we went into a pub called the Proud Salopian. Sitting there was this little chef from the cook house, so I mentioned the borrowing to Jack. He said, "I don't believe it!" He went straight over to him, lifted him out of the seat by his collar and took him to the toilet. After a little while, Jack returned and put twenty quid in my hand and said, "Don't get caught like that again!" We had a good night and turned out to be good friends afterwards.

Jack had served with the Parachute Regiment and he taught me everything I needed to know - how to make my bed box, how to 'bull' my boots, polish my brasses without getting cleaner all over my 'No.2s' and how to get the webbing just right. He explained the greatest mystery of all time - how to get a beret to fit nicely. (You must firstly soak the beret in water and whilst it is soaking, you set it on your head, then carefully remove it and place it on a hot-water radiator until it sets into place. It will fit just right!). He also explained how to deal with the cut of a uniform.

I was entranced by the stories Jack told me about the excitement of jumping out of aeroplanes and slipstreams…If you twisted yourself around when jumping out of the airplane door it would be possible to see the plane flying away from you - as I later discovered for myself. These tales made me even more determined to go into the Parachute Regiment (also known as '16th Airborne Brigade').

We were coming up to the fifth week of training in my new platoon. I was going to be trained on weapons such as the Self-loading Rifle and General Purpose Machinegun - both of which have 7.62 calibre barrels. In addition, we would be instructed in the use and maintenance of the LMG (Light Machine gun), otherwise known as the Bren Gun. This weapon had been converted from using 303 to 7.62 ammunition and had a magazine which held 32 rounds. It was extremely accurate (sometimes too accurate!) and we were expected to strip down and reassemble them in less than a minute.

All that the lads were talking about was that the following week we were due to go into the Gas Chamber which was situated at the rear of the camp. When the feared day arrived, we were all lined up outside in full battle -dress combat suits with full webbing, '44 Pack' and steel helmets, to make it more realistic. Gas mask in hand, we were taken four at a time through the steel door of what looked like an air raid shelter. Once we were all inside there, we were told to put our masks on and then the NCO would throw a gas canister in which would burst open with a small explosion and the gas would escape. After about two minutes, we were told to take our gas masks off. We were assured that there would be coughing and spluttering after another minute (it was to seem far longer)

But just when we thought we couldn't stand it any more, they would open the door and we could all run out, fall to the ground and try to get our breath back. It would take about ten minutes for us to recover. All of this was to show us what it would be like in a real gas attack. We never found out what type of gas it was, but we were all pleased when that particular little exercise was over.

The thing that we did not know as that it was now time for a little more exercise - a ten-mile run with the full kit on which we were still wearing and an assault course to follow! All of this was before lunch. In the afternoon we were introduced to the 9mm Sterling machine gun. This weapon was intended for close-quarter battle such as jungle warfare. It was easy to use with a 32 round magazine. Another day was nearly over and I remember that day well.

One particular night, we were confined to camp because the kit-inspection had not been up to standard that morning. The Platoon Sergeant went 'mental' and started turning lockers upside down - all because he found a pair of dirty socks in the bottom of one of the lockers. He promised us that if things were not as required by tonight, he would have another inspection as a punishment. At about 7.00pm that night, we were in a panic, trying to make sure that everything was as perfect as we could humanly manage. Then we heard a scream from the entrance of the barrack room, "STAND BY YOUR BEDS!!" from one of the two Corporals to be followed soon after by Platoon Sgt Hassle who would have another fit every hour until we got it to his satisfaction.

They found nothing wrong with the kit-inspection but everything ended up on the floor, inevitably, because the floor was not polished up to standard. They gave us another hour to put it right and if it was not as demanded by eight o'clock that night they guaranteed that it would be by nine o'clock! We got the polish out and two spread it on the floor whilst another two got busy with the 'bumpers' which were simple mechanisms composed of long, heavy, oblong pads which could be slid backwards and forwards by means of a long, hinged broom handle affair. By means of much labour, eventually, the polished floor would acquire a wonderful shine. By the time we could see our reflections on the floor and had had our inspection, very little time would be left for preparing our kit for the next morning. Some of us would be still there at midnight.

My training went on smoothly from then on and soon it was time for the final exercise in the bleak terrain of the Brecon Beacons of Wales - particularly Pen-y-Fan. There was to be no luxury of pre-built trenches. We had to dig them ourselves and put in sleeping bays slightly below ground level - all this in freezing weather! Fortunately, I didn't mind - I had been used to collecting sea-coal on the North East coast alongside my eldest brother Ernest in just such conditions. All my life I had been using a shovel in cold weather. My hands were hardened, as was my upper body strength from lifting shovelfuls of coal up above head height. I finished my trench well before anyone else and then could help out those on either side of my sleeping space. I had never heard so many moans and groans as came from all sides that day. If the aim of the course was to toughen the men, it certainly was succeeding.

The NCOs, to add a bit of mischief, waited until we had got well asleep - about three o'clock in the morning - and started chucking thunder-flashes about the place. Then the 'gimpy' (General Purpose Machine Gun) opened up firing blanks. All hell was let loose and we jerked from oblivion to nerve-tingling consciousness in three seconds, on guard and ready for action. We were all standing there in total darkness - not even able to see the man standing by your elbow. Suddenly a loud crack occurred and a para-illuminating flare shot high into the night sky, turning the night into an eerie daylight with shadows darting in all the wrong places. We would be on alert from then until six o'clock on a dark October morning as we watched the dew forming and freezing on the hillsides where even the sheep seemed to be shivering. At this point, the NCOs advised us that we were all going on a twelve mile forced march.

We had to leave the countryside as we found it - unbroken and tidy - so that the enemy would not be able to tell that we had been there. The march was far from a gentle stroll as you might take along a road, but up hill and down dale, up to our waists in water. All the while we could hear the roaring and grinding of fifty-odd tonnes of grating steel and armour plating barrelling down on our position. The platoon scattered in a controlled 'explosion' as the juggernaut Chieftain battle tank disappeared into the mist as quickly as it had appeared.

After gathering our wits again after the Chieftain 'tank assault', we were returned to our forced march with NCOs screaming all the while. Just as we were onto our last few miles, we began to cross a reasonably shallow river and were thankful that we could cool our feet, when our mentors shouted, "DOWN!" and we realised that, unbelievably, we were being ordered to lie down in the river. Still, it was all good fun. After we were all well soaked-through, the NCOs informed us that it was time to move on, only four miles to go (a 'walk in the park') and 'sarnies' and hot tea would await us. We thought lovingly of getting onto the transports when we would be taken back to Brecon Camp for a shower and a hot meal - then on to Shrewsbury barracks, or so we thought.

The 'walk in the park' turned out to be up and down Pen-y-Fan, which is almost ten thousand feet of Welsh mountain - a God-given endurance test! This appalling place was to mean 'make-or-break' and would sort out 'the men from the boys' on the course. We had climbed up, virtually on our hands and knees. When I reached the top and looked down, I could see some lads crawling and a few did not make it to the top because their feet were blistered and bleeding. I realised just how tough the mountain had made those of us who had survived.

It was the end of our training. We had completed all our tasks and it was time for a night out. To our surprise, we were escorted by our nasty NCOs, who turned out to be as human as the rest of us. Being hard on raw recruits was simply part of their job description. Now, that was all finished and we all went down to Brecon village and had a real good piss-up. For the first time we were allowed to call our NCOs by their first names. I don't think Cpl 'Nellie' Bassett took too kindly to us using the 'Nellie' bit. Ben Halliwell brought his Red Setter dog and what with him running his fingers through his long, curly moustache as he drank his pint, we found them to be quite human after all.

Chieftan tank

Lt. Col. Maughn and Captain Hall with 3 Platoon in the background

Chapter 4

Passout Parade / Leave cancelled / Singapore / Crossing the South China Seas / Ghurkas / Jungle Kit / Bali Ringin / The lads in the 'Stockade'

Thirty two of us had finished the course and we set off very early in the 4-tonners to get back to Copthorne Barracks where we all assembled in the gym. It seemed that we were waiting ages before we found out who had passed and who had failed. At last the Company Commander Major Lane entered, and read out the names. I couldn't believe it when he read out my name. After it was all over, we had a debriefing and were told how well we had done.

It was early November and approaching my birthday and we were looking forward to going home for Christmas leave. First came the Passing Out Parade which lasted about an hour and the C/O, Lieutenant Colonel Salisbury Trelawney, took the salute. We marched past with the band and bugles playing away. He was to inspect us and I thought he would get a bit of a shock when he saw that I had passed out, after our previous encounters. After it was all over, we returned to our barrack rooms, changed into our civvy clothes and went to collect our pay and travel warrants to go on 6-weeks' leave. However, the seven of us who were going to the Durham Light Infantry got a bit of a shock. We were told to stay in the barrack room for a briefing. Lenny March, Billy Hart, Durnall and myself, together with three others were paraded in front of the Company Commander Major Lane.

That was when we were told of the troubles in Malaya in the Far East and that all leave had been cancelled. We were on a 24hr standby to move to join our Battalion, who were already in the northern territories of Borneo, waiting to go into the troubled Sarawak area. I never imagined that I was to spend my Christmas in the Indonesian jungle and to come to within two or three feet of enemy troops in virtually hand-to-hand fighting. I would see some of my friends wounded and killed and wouldn't see my family again until the following June.

We handed in our kit to the stores. More would be issued to us when we went to join our regiment, the Durham Light Infantry - my county regiment. I was really proud and pleased when we were told that we would receive a medal for taking part in this campaign - the Borneo Campaign Service Medal with Clasp. A greater shock was awaiting me - I hadn't realised that we would have to put our lives in danger to get this award and that we would be going straight into 'the sharp end' into Sarawak and along the Indonesian border, which is the thickest jungle in the world. We were to join the advance party in Bali Ringin, as the main body of the Battalion were still in the northern territory. This was the area known as Sabah in North Borneo and it was on high alert.

The battalion was due to move down to this troubled region on active service to assist in what was called the 'Malaysian Conflict' between Indonesia and Malaya, and we would be serving alongside the SAS, the Ghurkas and the Royal Marine Commandos. The 2nd Parachute Regiment would be doing patrols into the Kalimantan jungle of Indonesia and along the 900-mile border of Sarawak. I had never heard of the place, as at the time there was never any publicity or any mention in the press about trouble in Borneo. It was all so secretive.

We were told that we had two days to prepare to leave for Singapore and had to have our vaccinations for all known diseases. Passports were issued and we were put on a 24hr movement order, confined to camp and allowed strictly no letters home to tell of our destination. This was a direct order from the officer in charge. We finally did move on the 12th November and took off from RAF Northolt for my first ever trip in an aeroplane. It was something else! Who would have thought that in a couple of years I would be jumping out of one of these aircraft! At the time, it was enough for me just to be looking out of the window. During our journey, I was thinking of Jack O'Connor whom I had left behind at the depot because he had been posted to the King's Own Yorkshire Light Infantry. I would miss him and his expert advice.

We landed in Colombo in Ceylon and the seven of us were told to leave the aeroplane. We went into the lounge area where we were instructed to stay. Lenny March, Billy Hart, Durnall and myself always stuck together. We had landed right in the middle of a terrorist situation and there were armed police and troops everywhere. Fighting broke out with sporadic firing here and there. There was panic everywhere and all we could do was take cover, keep our heads down and listen to the screaming and gunfire. After about 20 minutes, all went silent and I thought they must have got the situation under control. This was in fact the case and we managed to board the plane at last. After about two hours we were on our way to Kuala Lumpur - our last stop for refuelling before going on to Singapore, which we reached in about one hour. Finally, we were at the end of our journey.

When we arrived at the reception area, there were two red caps (military policemen) waiting to escort us to barracks. They called it the Nee Soon Garrison, where the famous Ghurka Rifles were stationed. They were well known for their heroics. We were told that these men could cut the boot laces of the enemy at night, in the jungle, before anyone realised that they were there.

After going through customs, we changed what little money we had left into Malaysian dollars and made sure that we had our pay books and passports with us. We had been told that we would receive one month's pay on arrival in Nee Soon camp. This was unlike barracks in the UK - it was like an old movie set, with wooden huts made from planks and corrugated sheets. There were no windows except for flaps, which could be lifted up on hot days to allow a cool breeze to waft through, though not much did. It was very hot and sticky. Inside was a bare wooden floor with standard army-issue steel beds and rock-hard mattresses, which told us that we were still in the army. Draped around the beds were mosquito nets to keep the little biting bastards away from our skin.

It was the twenty-first of November 1965 and my eighteenth birthday. I didn't even get a pint of beer. Stories were coming back to us that a gun battle was going on in Sarawak, between soldiers of the Ghurka Rifles and Indonesian troops. There had been fatalities, which made us determined to make the most of the couple of weeks during which Nee Soon camp was to be our home. This was the transit wing of the Far East Jungle Warfare Training Centre.

We were soon penniless and one of us had to ask the major I/C (In Command) if he could organise some pay for us. He did this very quickly and we were given four weeks pay, as promised - a total of twenty-two pounds and ten shillings (£22.50, equal to about £800 today). We were told that our next pay would be when we arrived in Kuching. It would include our over-seas allowance, which was an extra two pounds, seven shillings and sixpence (£2.37+) a week. As they could only give us what was marked in our pay books, we were all advised to allocate a small payment to our parents since we were about to go on active service. So I allocated ten shillings (50p a week) to my mother, because they let us know that if we didn't do something like this, it would be very difficult for our nearest and dearest to claim any compensation in the case of something happening to us. We were paid in dollars - but after a couple of nights in Nee Soon we were back at square one, skint. We had a lot to learn about Singapore and the value of money, but with the training that was ahead of us we would have little need for it. An advance party of the Ghurka Rifles was also there. They were just finishing a tour of duty in Borneo, which had not been without incident, and seemed to be immune to mosquitoes.

We were told to report to the Quartermaster's Stores to draw our jungle kit (tropical clothing) and were issued with two pairs of 'O.Gs'('jungle greens'), and two pairs of jungle boots which were made of canvas and laced up to just below the knee. In addition to this lot, we were given one 7.62 Self-Loading Rifle with two full magazines containing 20 rounds each. We went in front of a major from the Royal Greenjackets and he disclosed to us that we would be here for three weeks to get acclimatised and be taught all aspects of jungle warfare training in the time permitted.

We would be training alongside the Ghurkas who would be teaching us mine-warfare, booby-traps and how to survive in the jungle. This was tough training and I already knew what it was like to be hot and sweaty.

You would be soaking in a very short time, which was very unpleasant, and despite it being so very, very hot, we did not get much chance to relax. When we did go into town, it would be time to get back as there was a curfew and you had to be off the streets by 23.00hrs or risk getting locked up or even shot.

We were on our last week of training and handed our weapons into the arms stores. They would be reissued when we reached Borneo. On our last day in Singapore, we made a short journey by truck to the harbour where we boarded a large troop ship called the HMS W.W. Auby ('HMS Rust Bucket' - I had seen better ships than this being cut up in Hartlepool dry dock). As we climbed up the gangway of the ship, we saw men with trilbies which had a red band around them on their heads. They were the Ghurka Rifles who served in Borneo on permanent bases of company or battalion strength.

As the ship left the harbour, and we looked back to see the land disappearing into the distance, we felt exhilarated to think that we were on our way across the South China Sea. The voyage was not a good one. Due to the ship's rocking from side to side in the heavy seas, some of the lads were very sick and I didn't feel too good myself. When, later that night a film was being shown on deck, I tried to watch it but my head would start spinning as if I was on a Walzer ride at a fairground. After three days, we got our first sight of Borneo, which was to be our home for the next six months. I thanked God for the chance to get off this ship and onto dry land.

We disembarked from the troop ship 'HMS Rust Bucket' in awe and wonderment that it had not sunk in Kuching Harbour, leaving the company of Ghurkas which had come across from Singapore. They were now on their way to another camp further along the border. Although they were very small in stature, the Ghurkas looked very smart and were quietly proud - nice chaps, but 'ard as nails'.

The seven of us were told to report to Colour Sergeant Durham - a fitting name for a man who served in this regiment. He was in charge of stores and the reception and distribution of post and rations to the battalion. We drew all our kit and were amazed to find that everything was green even to our underpants. We got changed and left all our other clothing packed in a suitcase in the stores, since we would not need them where we were going. We were then issued with a 7.62mm SLR together with two magazines of 20 rounds. The colour sergeant told us to be alert and on our guard at all times. As soon as we got on those trucks we should be prepared for anything, snipers or ambush, and to treat anyone that looked Chinese as an enemy, until we were told otherwise. We all thought he was joking, but he was deadly serious.

Totty Taylor, M.T. Section

We boarded the four ton Bedford lorries for our trip to battalion H.Q., which was known as 'Balai Ringin' and was a long trip by road. We also had an escort of two Saracen Armoured Scout Cars in case of ambush. The Bedfords had their canvas sides rolled up, so we had an all-round view. The trip was a dusty one with the lorry travelling at least forty-five miles an hour along a long, dry and dusty road. We had to wrap our army-issue veils around our mouths and keep our bush hats pulled well down onto our heads. These lorries would do this run twice a week, delivering rations and ammunition to battalion H.Q., from where it was distributed to forward bases by helicopters. They called it the 'Milk Run'. In all, it was about sixty miles by road from Kuching to Bali Ringin near the Indonesian border.

We finally arrived at the camp and the driver jumped down from his cab with pressed 'O.G's' and looking very smart. The lads, covered in dust from the journey, began shouting at him about the rough ride they had just had. The driver, a Pte Taylor ('Totty') replied, "Sorry lads, but it's standing orders. The minimum speed is forty miles per hour in case of an ambush." The guard post constructed at the entrance was sandbagged and had a GPMG covering all the front of the camp. On the road that ran past the camp, we could see the RAF ground crews maintaining the Wessex Whirlwinds and Belvederes and all wearing shorts and pairs of flip-flops in the hot sun. The next thing I noticed was the Provost Sgt, a

Maintenance on the 5.5 guns

Sgt Knowles (nicknamed 'Chatty Knowles'), waiting at the gate as the lorry entered. He had a long moustache curled up both sides of his face and he was watching his NCO with two prisoners. Everywhere they went in that hot sun, they were double-marched. It was a shock to me when I realised that one of them was an old mate from my home town. This was one of the lads who had told me to join up and how much of a good time he was having. It was Brian Constable, always getting into scrapes, but he could handle it all. I tried to catch his attention and talk to him but the provo-sergeant was having none of it.

I found out later that Brian had got involved in a fight and had been awarded fifty six days in the guard room (out here they called it the 'stockade'). The best and worst of it was that all I could remember of Brian were the good times down at the Queen's Rink and the battles outside with the colliery lads.

The other prisoner was a lad named Wally Kidd and strangely, he was also from Hartlepool. He was serving one hundred and twelve days for being absent without leave. It seemed to me that the Hartlepudlians were not having much luck in this battalion. I asked myself if it was all really worth it - because I, for one, had learned my lesson once and for all and would never be going in there again!

I was shocked as we looked around the camp. We could see two 105 Howitzers and a 4.2 inch mortar in pits in the centre of the camp. There were guard posts at each corner of the camp - enough fire-power to deal with any attack outside the camp. The trees were cut down for some 30 metres and replaced with coils of barbed wire, something like an assault course with trip-flares and booby-traps. The huts were constructed of wood and corrugated sheets and one of these was to be my home for the next two or three weeks.

Making a birouac for the night on jungle patrol

Chapter 5

Commence 6-month tour of Borneo / Jungle Warfare Training / 3-day Patrols / River Boats / Man Overboard / Unarmed Combat Training / A Black Scorpion / RSM 'Florrie'

There were still members of the Royal Greenjackets' party waiting to go home. They were quite friendly, or maybe they were just relieved to be getting out. The advance party of the Durham Light Infantry was also there - parts of HQ Company, such as clerks and the Assault Pioneer Platoon, because the main body was still in the northern area of Borneo and ready to relieve the Royal Greenjackets.

The seven of us were told to parade at the company office for a briefing from the adjutant. It was more like a potted history of Borneo - how the undeclared war had started. Britain had two colonies on this island, Sarawak and Sabah and gave protection to the Sultanate of Brunei in Malaya. The former British colony was working hard for the formation of a new political entity, in the region to comprise Sarawak, Sarawak Brunei, Malaya and Singapore. It was titled *The Federation of Malaysia* and was regarded by Britain and her allies as a valuable bulwark against the perceived threat of Communist China in the region. However, president Sukarno of Indonesia was opposed to the idea of the Federation as he thought it was a cloak for continued British influence in an area that had hard-won its independence from the British Empire, and as such threatened his ambitions in Indonesia.

A Chinese guerrilla group, mostly based in the Sarawak region, was similarly opposed to the Federation and they had contacts in many areas. Sukarno supplied them with weapons and allowed them to train in the Indonesian Kalimantan jungle of Borneo. They then infiltrated into Sabah and Sarawak. The capital of Indonesia, Jakarta, was in a state of emergency with rioting, executions, murder, looting and The emergency evacuation of all British and American personnel from the country had taken place.

We were also told that during our six-month tour of duty in Borneo, we stood a very good chance of coming face to face with the enemy, Chinese or Indonesian guerrillas, on our patrols. The next three weeks would be very important to our survival in the Borneo jungle because it was a continuation of our training course in Singapore and was to include training on assault boats used on the long stretches of river - a nerve-wracking experience.

That night, around six, we were relaxing after changing into shorts, when I heard one loud bang after another and I thought we were being attacked. The lads told me not to panic as the artillery was accustomed to firing twenty rounds from the howitzers at targets along the border every night.

Training would start the following morning when we would meet our NCOs. While we were in the camp we would receive basic instruction in radio -operation, weapons and jungle-survival techniques. We would be doing three-day patrols into the jungle with Cpl Muir and Lance Cpl Seed, both of whom were Geordies. Seed was a small man whereas Muir was a dark-skinned, giant of a man, whose bark was worse than his bite and who was very experienced in jungle warfare. He told us that they had just returned from a jungle-warfare school in Bangkok and that he and other instructors in the camp would be training us for three weeks. On patrol, we would be taught how to build a bivouac to keep us reasonably dry during the heavy downpours or monsoon rains.

When it did pour down, all we could do was sit underneath lightweight ponchos and hope they did not collapse on us with the weight of water that was crashing down on us and running between our feet. We couldn't even hear a conversation for the noise in between the storms, but the rain would stop as fast as it had begun and we could dry out very quickly in open ground under the blazing hot sun that would follow.

As we dried out, our NCO would tell us stories to get his point over, one of which comes to mind immediately. One of our predecessors, a member of the Royal Greenjackets, had stood on an anti-personnel mine known as a 'Dingbat' - one of the most vicious anti-personnel mines, quite capable of removing your legs from the knees.1965 also saw the Indonesian raiders introduce simple wooden 'cigar-box' anti-personnel mines along the border tracks. This added a macabre and sickly note into patrolling and a number of legs and feet were lost.

Over the next three weeks, we did three-day patrols that seemed like three weeks, to teach us survival and to be on the constant look-out for enemy booby-traps. Whilst on patrol, we were told that our worst enemy lay at our feet because we might step on or a trip a wire. We must always look on the ground in front with every step we took but not to ignore what might be above. During the next few days, we were to report to a Cpl. Wardrobe and a Lance Cpl. Norton of the Assault Pioneer Platoon who would introduce us to the river patrols.

We used army assault boats, which had powerful outboard motors. They were sixteen feet in length and were built to carry about twelve men with full equipment. The really hard bit was the launching of these boats, which had to be

River patrol

carried between us at the double to the water's edge. We would then run into the water until we were waist-deep and jump into the craft as the water got deeper and we could start the motor to cruise along the river at speed with an Iban guide.

These waters must be patrolled with caution, even though we had a GPMG mounted on the front of the boat and we would spread ourselves out along the bottom of the boats to make as small a target as possible. It was terrifying. We couldn't take our eyes away from the water's edge or from the trees in the surrounding jungle. We didn't know what to expect at every bend and twist in the river because the fact was that if we got ambushed along this river we would stand no chance of survival.

We could not wait to get back on dry land, and the fear gripping our stomachs would disappear the minute our feet touched solid earth. All we wanted was to get our heads under the cover and protection of the dense undergrowth. During these patrols, the NCOs would appear not to be at all bothered - though they could have just been hiding their fear.

On one occasion, we were heading towards the river bank at the end of a patrol and the point man at the front was another Hartlepudlian, Billy Hart. He had the anchor rope firmly gripped in his hand as he prepared to jump onto the riverbank to anchor the boat on the command of Cpl.Wardrobe. We all heard the order and Billy jumped without hesitating, only to disappear into the water in front of our eyes. We couldn't believe what we were seeing - but what we could not see was

Billy. We could feel the bottom of the boat hitting him as we went forward. Lenny March crouched opposite and wondered what was happening. I didn't wait but immediately jumped into the water to find Billy being sucked under the water towards the spinning propeller blades, which were now about two feet away. I grabbed him by the webbing and his shirt, pulled him out from under the boat and dragged him to the water's edge. Billy was trying to catch his breath and spewing water as he recovered. He and the NCO soon realised that his rifle was missing and that it must still be at the muddy bottom of the river. To loose a rifle was a chargeable offence, and Billy knew that he had to go back into the deep, dark, fast-flowing river to recover his weapon. He did so without any hesitation.

As it turned out, these men really knew what they were doing and were well trained, even though the order to jump had been given a bit too early. Everyone makes mistakes, though this one could have cost a life. Over and over again, the procedures were repeated until they knew we had taken it all in. We were questioned and told that it was all for our own good, preparing us for future border patrols.

In addition, we were taught the finer points of unarmed combat with only a bayonet for protection. Our instructors would command us to attack them with the bayonet above our heads and to charge them with vigour, really trying to hurt them (as if!) We would be lying prone before you could say, "Bob's your uncle!" After this humiliation, the instructors would allow us to be the defenders and try to put them on their backs by trapping the hand with the weapon between our crossed wrists and then to sweep their feet from beneath them. It was harder than it looked with me being ten stone weight and Chalky White being fifteen stone. Just as with learning to dance, we were shown how to move with careful grace towards the unbelievable conclusion when our instructors would be lying prone on the ground, unarmed and beaten as we had been.

We learned other things such as straining and sterilising water before drinking it, and where to find water when there was none easily to be found. One technique was to open a pitcher plant and strain the insects from the liquid inside. It had a slightly bittersweet taste to it, but at a pinch, it would save your life. Protection against mosquitoes and other insects could be gained by smearing mud across your arms and any open patch of skin - all tools to be made use of when all other avenues were exhausted.

I had a terrifying experience and a narrow escape a few days later whilst in Bali Ringin, when a black scorpion got onto my shoulder. I was at the entrance to one of the guard posts and was leaning against the doorpost when one of the lads saw it. I thought he was joking, then I felt it move and I was terrified. I went rigid as I watched Corporal Seed draw his machete from his webbing. After telling me to remain still, he brushed it from my shoulder to the ground. That taught me not to lean against anything again. It must have crawled down the doorway and onto my shoulder. If I had not been wearing my jacket, things might have been very different. I was wondering if these things only happened to me. Corporal Seed said, "That's another thing to look out for. A scorpion can be as deadly as the enemy!"

During the day, you were allowed to walk about in shorts, but you still had to carry your weapon, with two full magazines, at all times and a full bottle of drinking water on your webbing belt. The lads and I were 'skint'. It was early evening and one of the lads said that if we were hungry, we should go and see the 'Cha Walla' and he would give us a bacon and egg 'banjo' each 'on the strap'. We thought he was kidding but we thought we would give it a try. Off we went to see the 'Cha Walla' and he told us that, yes, we could have a bacon and egg banjo and 'put it on the slate' until payday. He said, "Very well sir. You are a very good man!" and there were the banjos in front of us. We gave our names and he put them in a book. The Colour Sergeant made sure he got his money and the 'Cha Walla' gave him free tea and sandwiches as a small commission. I thought it was a great idea.

Next day we had it easier with some weapons-training all morning. We had to strip our rifles down and reassemble them within a time limit. They made sure that we would know everything before we were sent up the 'Sharp End'. The wearing of shorts together with webbing, water bottle and the carrying of one's weapon at all times regime continued, although we had to wear our shirts to protect ourselves against the sun, which was very strong. We had this constant reminder that we were only a little way above the equator. If you were caught by the sun, not only was it very painful, but you would be put on a charge for 'Self-Inflicted Wounds'.

During the day, you always knew when Sergeant Major Ford was on his rounds, because everyone made themselves scarce. 'Florrie'; as we nicknamed him because of his large feet, heels together and toes six inches apart; would always find you a job if he saw you wandering about looking idle. He bore an uncanny resemblance to 'RSM Claude Snudge' from the TV. Programme 'Bootsie & Snudge' of the time. There were many occasions when he was in one of his 'moods'. He would parade the company on the helipad and march you up and down till you nearly dropped. This included even the rear party of the Royal Greenjackets, although they weren't in our regiment. He didn't care what cap badge they were wearing, they were still in the British Army and were marched up and down at an excruciating 180 paces.

A little incident comes to mind. I remember one day, a local mongrel ran onto the helipad whilst we were all on parade. With a playful glint in its eyes, it savaged Florrie's puttees! As we were marching, all you could hear was, "LEFT, RIGHT ... GEROUT OF IT! LEFT, RIGHT ... GEROUT OF IT!!" The entire parade was in stitches. However, the RSM wasn't amused. It was a relief to see finally a helicopter hovering above us because that meant clearing the helipad to enable it to land.

Leaving Bali Ringin

Emergency field dressing on patrol

Chapter 6

Accidental discharge of GPMG / Flying beetles / Spraying with 'Defoliants/ Leaving Balai Ringin / Helicopter to 'Gunin Gadja' / Boxers in 'No.1 Platoon'/ Getting to know the lads in my platoon.

It was in the middle of the afternoon, when an incident at the guard post shocked all of us. The sentry post opposite the observation post was in use when a civilian truck approached. The sentry decided to stop it and walked forward to do a spot check. He was covered at all times by another sentry on the opposite side of the road who was on duty in the sandbagged bunker armed with a GPMG, which was usually on 'Sustained Fire Role'.As the sentry told the driver to get out, the machinegun opened up, cutting the sentry box totally in half. A chainsaw couldn't have done a better job. The other sentry on the gun position froze with his finger on the trigger. Someone had taken the safety catch off. It was very fortunate for the soldier who had decided to do the spot check at that moment. Everybody realised what must have happened and he was arrested for the first accidental discharge in Borneo by anyone in the battalion. Then it was back to normal duties.

I was on guard that night at a sentry post at the far end of the camp. It was normal practice that two of us would be on duty all night armed with a GPMG and a box of what were known as the 'Thirty Six' hand grenade.

We had a radio for reporting every hour to the CP. and binoculars. We spent all night just looking at the barbed wire and as far back as the trees, seeing some strange animals. Many types of lizard scuttled onto the sandbags about two or three feet in front of us, staring with their large eyes as if we were not there. The flying beetles didn't rest until it was dark and then the fireflies would take over - millions of them. I had never heard such strange noises in my entire life. It was frightening and I told myself that I wouldn't be sorry when this night came to an end. Of course, it was just a matter of getting used to these strange surroundings. First light would come in very quickly, about 05.30.

Usually, if an attack was going to come, this would be the likeliest time, so it was 'on alert' and 'standing to' when daylight was here and the first stirrings of activity could be heard on camp. The strange wildlife would appear and quite often you would feel a sudden thump in the back by a flying beetle; something like a huge cockroach. They would hit anything that got in their way and the Sergeant Major was no exception because everybody got their turn. We would hear muttered swear-words and would know that someone else had been hit by one of these strange beetles.

It was at this time at the camp received some important visitors, as was later reported in the DLI Regimental Journal no. 101 of June 1966: *"Mr Cornford, Chief Scientist to the army, and Mr Herbert, an expert on weedkilling (defoliation is the polite term) came in February"*. This visit sounded innocuous enough, but it heralded events that still cast a long shadow today. Shortly after this visit scores of canisters and spray equipment arrived in the camp. A light aircraft sprayed the area way beyond the defence perimeter of the camp, and our soldiers were also set to work spraying it over the undergrowth, and setting up trip flares among the trees. The protection which the soldiers were given against the toxic spray seemed to be completely inadequate: nothing more than a piece of cloth to protect the nose and mouth. The results of this spray were dramatically effective. The lush foliage of the jungle died completely in a matter of days, leaving a clear "killing area" in front of the camps. We wouldn't see any wildlife for several days. At least they had some sense: Brian Constable who had been applying the spray confided to John Taylor: "with anything that works as quickly as that, there have to be repercussions." Brian Constable died of cancer at the early age of 42.

It is now known that a form of the notorious toxic herbicide Agent Orange had already been tried out by the British army in Malaya in the 1950s, where it was found to be particularly effective in tropical climates. Agent Orange was used to devastating effect by the US army in Vietnam two years after the Borneo conflict, and was sprayed not only over jungle cover but rice paddies, crop fields, lakes and rivers. As early as 1963 reports had begun to appear in the U.S. press linking cancer in laboratory mice with the dioxins in Agent Orange and similar herbicides. It was suggested that there might be significant health risks for people handling such chemicals. The US media largely ignored these reports and it is not certain to what extent it was known in Britain by 1966 what effects these defoliants would have on the soldiers' health. What I do know is that hundreds of soldiers who fought in that region at the time have died early deaths of cancer and cancer-related illnesses. The matter has still not been adequately investigated.

We were told that our stay in this camp was coming to an end and that we should be prepared to move to the forward base camps over the next two days. We had a briefing from the Commanding Officer, a Lieutenant Colonel Maughan, to let us know what was expected of us before we left. The Colour Sergeant would ensure that we all squared-up with the 'Char Wallah' so that his future 'commission' supplies of free cheese and onion sarnies and cups of hot tea would be ensured. Our stay at Balai Ringin had come to an end. I was told I would be going to 'A' Company at Guning Gadja, together with Lenny March and Durnall. Billy Hart was going to 'B' Company based at Pluman Mapu. This did worry us a bit because we were bound for the most troublesome spots for the whole battalion. When the rest of the lads found out where I was going, they told us stories all that night about what had happened to the Commandoes and the Parachute Regiment in their contacts with the enemy. If they were just trying to put the 'shits' up us, they succeeded.

Next morning, we boarded the Wessex Whirlwind helicopter because, we were told, there was no road and the base camp we were going to was close to the border. The only means of getting there was by chopper. The Regimental Sergeant Major did all the marshalling of air flights in and out to ensure that everything was done by the book and that no mistakes were made. 'Florrie' the RSM, a man of about six feet, well-built, aged about forty five to fifty and balding, used to run about like a twenty year old. After a journey of about 15 minutes, we arrived at Kampong Bunan Gega (which we nicknamed 'Gunin Gadja' for ease of pronunciation).

The helicopter circled a huge hill, making sure of a safe approach and at the helipad it did not land but hovered about three feet off the ground. We then had to jump with all our kit on. When I recovered myself, I waited for the dust cloud to clear, then as the helicopter clattered off into the distance, I looked around and saw the camp. It was unbelievable - just as if we had jumped into the middle of an old war movie. The first thing that made us open our eyes was the amount of barbed wire and then the number of strongholds constructed of sandbags. You could see the muzzles of the machineguns sticking out of the observation posts and a guard with binoculars on lookout. The artillerymen were standing by their howitzers which were also surrounded by sandbag walls for protection. The 105 gun was in the middle, with shells stacked neatly close by at the ready as the helicopter landed.

Durnall, Lenny March and I were told to report to '1'Platoon, which was under the command of Lieutenant Bond and his subordinate Sgt.Charleton. As we entered his quarters, we found ourselves having to descend some steps because it was a room under the guard post. It had sandbagged walls and a single fold-up camp bed to one side, with all his kit and webbing at the foot. Maps were pinned to the walls and it was a cause of wonder for me that they managed to keep it so tidy. I didn't know at the time that these officers each had a personal batman who cleaned up after them and did all their running about for them. It was obvious that they had just returned from patrol.

We were told that training was over now and it was time to get down to some serious business. For the first few days we should get to know the lads and the layout of the camp. Before we left, he said, "I don't have to remind you that you are on active service now and there is a completely new set of rules now, so listen to your platoon sergeants and corporals and a Lance Corporal Patterson.

When the briefing was over, I was told to stay behind and Lt. Bond asked me to clean his armalite - give it a pull-through and oil it. As this was a direct order from an officer, though put politely, and since I was new to the battalion, I couldn't refuse. So I took his Armalite M15 up on top where I could see in the daylight. Since I had very little experience with this weapon, I really took it away to get some advice on how to strip it down. Nearby, I saw two men, heavily-tanned, repairing one of the sandbagged bunkers. I approached them and struck up a conversation with them. Their names were Allen Barella and Bob Griffiths, and they had just returned off patrol with the rest of their platoon and they were very helpful. Allen stripped it down in a matter of seconds and taught me how to clean it with a pull-through, and oil it.

This weapon was made of aluminium and had a plastic butt and stock. It was so light you could lift it with one finger. I had only known these men for thirty minutes but we got on so well that they were 'taking the piss' out of me already for cleaning Lt. Bond's rifle. Allen said that if I didn't want the job I should just have told him - he wouldn't have minded. They told me that they had just returned from a reconnaissance patrol and they all had still to clean their weapons. I mixed amongst the lads, trying to have some conversation that morning when I met Pte ('Bronco') Hoare who was the Lightweight Boxing Champion of the battalion. He was a small, quiet lad and he told me that Pte Alan Barella, Pte Murphy and Pte Bassett were all boxers. As '1 Platoon' was known for its boxers, I felt more at home and it encouraged me. These were the men I wanted to be with and, since they actually liked me, I fitted in with them.

It was lunch time and we went to the cookhouse with our mess tins and tin cup and with our rifles over our shoulders. As we entered, the other lads ('veterans') would call us 'Sproggies' which meant 'newcomers', and we had to put up with it. As I had just turned eighteen, I was the youngest soldier on the base.

Whilst in the cookhouse, you would hear noises every couple of minutes like a chicken or some other farmyard animal. The author of this chorus turned out to be Pte Keith Hope, another joker from Hartlepool! Always happy and smiling, this man turned out to be some character. If you walked past him in camp, he would always make some sort of animal noise or some other prank or joke on us newcomers. The rest of the platoon found it very funny. They were used to his practical jokes.

There were three sets of brothers in the company; Tony and Alan Barella from Pennywell, Sunderland, Bob and Tommy Griffiths from Shotton Colliery, County Durham, and Dennis and little ('Geordie') George Lawton, who was the shortest man in the company. He was one of the funniest with his jokes and his 'broad Geordie' accent. I couldn't understand a word he was saying at first, but when I got so that I could nearly understand him, he told me he was from Chester le Street, Co. Durham - only eighteen miles from Hartlepool! I was shocked to think of the enormous difference in dialect in that short distance, but since he understood me perfectly, that was all right.

During my first few weeks, we were to get no cash pay and everything we got from the NAAFI; for beer, chocolate or cigarettes we would have to sign a little chitty. We had to report to the Colour Sergeant Fawcett or his skivvy 'Shorty' Johnson, who was a right little Hitler. He helped distribute the beer and cigs and saw that we signed a form for every last thing we received, so that it could be deducted from our pay. What was left went into our 'credits' and we could draw the balance at the end of our tour of duty - something like a bank - on our return to England.

I was to share sleeping accommodation with Pte Miller, Pte Raey, Pte Durnall and Pte Cooper, a very quiet, friendly man who kept to himself and stayed on in the army after his demob date was up. At first, I had to be the 'gopher' ('go-fer-this-an'-that') and do all the running about, until one day, Miller had had a couple more Tiger Beers than he should have had and grabbed me by the dog-tags around my neck, nearly choking me. I thought to myself that I had been lucky back at the depot and I wasn't going to take another chance of going on a charge. So I prepared myself to take a good beating if I had to keep my fists to myself and wait for what was coming. I knew that I would almost certainly be thrown out of the army or get a couple of months in the stockade if I fought back, and I was not going to allow this to happen.

Then the penny dropped. I realised that he knew what had happened in the depot! One of the lads who had come over with us had opened his mouth. It was not difficult to figure out when I saw Durnall sitting on his camp bed close by. I said nothing at this juncture, as the last thing I wanted was trouble. He threatened that if ever I tried to be a hard case, I would have to go through him first. That is when Pte Barella came to my rescue and said, "Come on Geordie! Leave it, and we'll put Kelly on the boxing team when we get back to Blighty." I had never been so happy to see this tall, well-built man crouching, almost kneeling, as he held the hessian sack that covered the entrance above his head. Miller replied that they were only having a laugh, but it had not seemed like that to me at the time. It turned out that Barella was an army champion and was well-respected.

I also realised that it was this same Allan Barella who had helped me to clean the Platoon Commander's weapon a few days before. We became good friends and I got on quite well with Miller also after that little incident. However, I made a quick move of sleeping quarters because I wasn't prepared to take any chances, especially when Miller had had a few cans of beer. I took the spare bed space with Barella and Noble and a lad called Bob Griffiths, who had become friendly with me from the word go'. Bob was also a quiet man who kept to himself and I was surprised how well I got on with him. It was probably because of my age because from that time on we worked together on guard duties and cleaning weapons. He showed me the tricks of making life easier in this camp that looked like something out of the Second World War in Burma, with its trenches and bunkers on this huge hill.

Gunin Gadja - the layout of the camp

A Wessex delivering the post to Gunin Gadja

Chapter 7

Welsh Lads/ Iban Trackers / 'Hearts and Minds' Patrol / Codeine and Aspirin / Firing the Howitzer / Enemy Troop Movements Reported / On Patrol in the Jungle /Cliffs, Waterfalls, Climbing, Leeches and Ants

Because these three men were so tough, I felt honoured to be in their company. They were well-known and I noticed that every five minutes, someone would be calling in to our accommodation bringing cigarettes, chocolate or even the odd can of beer and were never asked where they came from. We would usually get visitors from the top of the camp where the Welsh had their accommodation. They were a platoon from the South Wales Border Regiment (Call sign '88') who were attached to us to make up the strength of the company. They were all good lads. Who was it who said that the Welsh and the Geordies don't mix ? We got on very well as the best part of these lads were from the valleys of South Wales were used to roughing it.

Close to our bunker was where the Iban trackers were accommodated. There were four of them, all covered in tattoos, and recruited from the local tribes as guides to and from the border regions. Each carried a Remington pump action shotgun issued by the British army and a long knife called a 'perang' as protection. One tracker was allocated to each platoon.

We were to leave the next day at first light for a 'day out', if you could call it that. It was what was referred to as a 'Hearts and Minds' mission. This is when we would take the duty medic with us and visit all the kampongs of the different tribes in the area of the base. It was a patrol to help the sick natives who would all stand in line, waiting for the 'wonder drug' which they all thought they would be getting. Codeine or aspirin seemed to work anyway, because the information we were getting out of them about enemy movement was reliable. We would surround every village we came to and clear the area, then they would parade in their traditional dress and wearing swords. The down side however was that there really was disease and it wasn't hard to understand why, since there was neither hospital nor doctor available and only their local 'medicine man' to turn to.

We had visited three villages by mid-afternoon. It was getting late and time that we were heading back to base. So we started on the long patrol home - as far as I was concerned, we had struggled through swamps and paddy fields just to give

Inspection before the start of a patrol

these tribesmen some aspirin. However, we fought our way through the thick jungle where the canopy of the trees restricted the sun's rays from ever touching the ground, the annoyance from the mosquitoes was incessant in the eternally damp atmosphere. We constantly slapped face or neck in a vain effort to catch the insect that had just bitten us, but there was always another myriad to take its place.

As we approached the river at the bottom of the hill, below our camp, the women from the kampong would be doing their laundry, slapping the at the rocks and just staring at us. Pat McGurk would make some usually funny crack about them and the lads would be having a laugh as we started climbing the steps to the camp. At last, having arrived back at base, we stood down and the sergeant reported back to Major Arnot to give the information we had collected that day.

Next day, we met Major Jag Arnot, our Company Commander. He was a chap of medium height, very calm but fond of the odd laugh and joke. He would usually walk round dressed very smartly in pressed OGs and carrying a side arm that looked like a Browning 9mm pistol. About forty years old, he had worked his way through the ranks and had served in Korea in 1952 and 1953. He had also been in the Royal Nigerian Army. He had accepted an emergency commission during 1946 and 1947, rising to the rank of lieutenant. He would speak to almost everyone who went by and even have conversations with private soldiers. There was no reason to avoid him. He was what you might call a gentleman: well -respected. He would usually come and watch us play 5-aside football on the helipad.

That is where I met my namesake 'Kelly 26' (I was 'Kelly 04') who was in '2 Platoon' and had a stammer which was so bad that we could hardly understand him, but he played football like another George Best. Everybody enjoyed watching 'Kelly 26' because his skills were wonderful. Miller, Donaldson and I also got on very well. Miller was about my build and as hard as nails. He seemed to take me under his wing and never mentioned the day he grabbed me around the neck again. We became very good friends.He told me that the main body of the company would be coming in the next few days and that we would see some changes. He never talked about his family - all he really spoke of was what he and Donaldson had got up to in Hong Kong. Miller told me that Mick Donaldson had once been a corporal but been 'busted' down to the rank of private for fighting in a bar in Kowloon, Hong Kong, with the Argyle and Southern Highlanders. He had floored two or three before being arrested and charged.

Anyway, this day was nearly done and after lying in the sun all afternoon, we were looking forward to the NAAFI. We were watching the artillery section,under the command of Major Atkins, order their howitzers into action before firing at targets over the border. They were under the supervision of Sergeant Batty, L/Bdr. Bowden and Gunners Stokes, Walton, Millward, Mitchell, Bromley and last of all, Mulloy. They certainly knew what they were doing and it was a sight to see as they loaded the huge shells into the breach and fired. We could feel the ground vibrating under our feet as every round was fired and rejoiced that we weren't on the receiving end of that lot.

That evening, whilst we were having a couple of cans, the platoon commander came in to join us and we were told that there had been a report of troop movements up by the border. Since we had no-one in that area, we had to consider this as being an enemy threat. We were told to prepare to move to investigate and that we would be moving at first light.

The following morning we assembled at the CP (Command Post) at first light, ready to move out. First of all, however, the platoon commander would inspect each one of us to make sure that we had everything we would need on this patrol. Arms, equipment and radio set were checked thoroughly as if anything was left behind when we set out would imperil the mission. The first man, always 'on point' duty would be an Iban tracker carrying his 12-bore Remington pump-action shotgun. You couldn't mistake one of these chaps. He would be covered from head to foot in raised tattoos - not drawn with ink, but cut deeply into the skin and stained with vegetable dyes.

The second man was the lead scout 'Thackeray' who was the one man who had to be alert at all times. In all, there would be 26 of us, including one Royal Signals operator who always carried an SMG. This weapon was a Sterling Machine Gun with, usually, a magazine of 32 rounds of 9mm calibre, designed for close-quarter

**Left - right: Lawrence Garroway (Gat), Charlie Bassett, Bob Noble,
Olson and D.K. (Durnall) at the end of a patrol**

combat and ideal for jungle warfare. As we left the stronghold, I wondered what lay before us. We seemed to be descending those steps for at least thirty minutes and when we got to the bottom, there was a fast-flowing river about twenty metres wide. On a bad day, after rainfall, it could be ten feet deep, but on another it would have only a few feet of depth and it would be possible to walk across the riverbed. The route we usually took involved crossing a long tree trunk, which spanned the width of the river from one side to the other and had a handrail of bamboo.

Once across, there was a small village and as we walked through, all the villagers and children would stare at us as if they had never seen a soldier before. In front of us there was an open space for about two hundred metres that we use as a DZ (Dropping Zone) for air-dropped supplies. We always made our way around the edge of the tree line to avoid the open space and then we would simply disappear into the mass of trees which was the commencement of the Borneo jungle for us. We would advance along the jungle track that the natives and other patrols had used many times before us, spread out three metres apart. This was a direct order from the platoon commander, so that we wouldn't provide easy targets for the enemy.

Because it had been trodden so frequently, the ground was fairly hard and we Geordies named it the 'A1'. We knew it would probably be safe from booby traps as it was used daily by the locals, but all the same, we stayed alert and advanced with great caution. It wasn't hard to work out that it would be a perfect place for an

Ken Jackson testing a GPHG

ambush. We often thought that if we were ever caught on this track we would be cut to pieces. We just hoped that if the commander knew this, the enemy did not!

As we went along, we would often meet native women, smiling all over their faces and chattering on in their own lingo which we couldn't understand, their bare breasts bouncing in front of them. On their backs they carried large baskets which were pointed at one end, and eighteen inches wide open at the other. As usual, it was the women who did all the carrying. When they did pass, you would hear one of the lads asking if we fancied this or that one and then would come McGurk's voice declaring, "No thanks. You can have her!" We were all sure that they kept all the good-looking women locked up at home...

All we could do was advance slowly along the track, looking in every direction for any movement in the trees and straining our ears to detect any odd sound. This was part of the patrol nobody liked. To put it politely, we were "shitting ourselves" and devoutly wishing we were "off this fucking track!" We followed it for about 1,000 metres then came upon a kampong (a little village whose 'long houses' were made out of bamboo and raised on stilts, so that the monsoons would not flood them out.) The roofs had tropical leaves to shoot the rain off and each structure had its own lean-to had a sort of balcony, where the kids stood staring at us with large eyes.

As we approached, we realised that it was as an Iban village and our tracker told us that three days previously there had been four armed strangers who they

Out on patrol with (c to r): "Brownie", an Iban tracker, and Bob Noble

thought were Indonesian or Chinese. He said that they had headed back towards the border, so we followed the track they had made, still on the lookout for mines or booby traps. The mist had come down like a blanket of fog and we could just make out the lead scout waving a piece of bamboo in front of him as he advanced. We soon realised that he was making sure that he wasn't going to walk into a trip wire.

It was slow but safe progress. We followed this track for two days until we came to the border and contacted base camp by radio, hoping to be told to return, but this wasn't to be. We had a climb in front of us of about 1,000 feet and because the platoon commander decided to go on up the border, we were given a thirty-minute rest period before starting out again.

Those thirty minutes seemed like two. We didn't even have time to take our '44 pack' off our backs and we were on our feet again and ready to continue with our patrol. One minute we would be in thick jungle and the next on open ground. There were cliffs, and the sound of running water hitting rocks. I couldn't explain what lunatics would try to cross this terrain, but we were those lunatics, wading through rivers and waterfalls, terrified we would be washed away or even drowned. Once across, we could see the cliff side with trees growing out of the side and streams of water gushing down from them.

We had one 'fucking great climb' ahead of us and knew that we wouldn't be able to rest on the way because it was far too steep. When it rained, the ground turned

On jungle patrol

into a quagmire. You were climbing up five metres and sliding back two, often grabbing at each other only to hear roars of: "Fucking get off me!" It was sometimes unavoidable because it was too easy to grab the back pack of the man in front of you. Sometimes, grasping a branch to pull oneself up, it would snap and you would finish up ten or twelve feet back down the steep hill having taken two of your mates with you. We were all covered in mud and wet through. We could feel the leeches embedding themselves into our flesh. The ants, being under the impression that they were being invaded by an enemies, came swarming out of their underground nests and commenced 'biting the fuck out of us'. We had to ignore all of this until we got back to our RV (rendez-vous).

Sometimes we would dig the butts of our weapons into the ground to get some sort of hold, to prevent us sliding back down. We wondered what on earth we were doing in this hell hole of a jungle.

We had been out nearly three days and were nearing the top of the border. We walked alongside the old tracks, probably made by other patrols, and the Indonesians knew this. If they thought we were using these tracks regularly, they would booby-trap them and did so on several occasions.

Quite often, a hand signal would be passed through the platoon to stop, then we would just crouch down with our rifles across our knees, looking into the thick jungle until it was judged safe to move on. Then we moved along carefully and with renewed caution.

Although we were supposed to be on the Sarawak side of the border, we regularly strayed into Indonesian territory. We tried to be as silent as possible and keep clear of twigs of bamboo that lay on the ground because they would snap and make the noise of a fire cracker. If there was an enemy in the area, they would hear this and it would give away our position. Make no mistake about it; it was something like firing a single round from a rifle.

Alan Barella and Bob Noble in the jungle waiting for the airdrop, early February 1966

Chapter 8

By this time it was obvious to us that we had crossed the border and were into enemy territory. We came across old slit trenches where some sort of confrontation had obviously taken place. Our platoon sergeant told us that it was here that Lance Corporal Rambahadur Limbu of the 2/10 Ghurkas had won the Victoria Cross (on 21 November, 1965) on a 'Claret' operation which was top secret and when they were well into Indonesian territory in the Kalimantan Jungle. L.Cpl. Limbu was in an advance party of 16 Ghurkas when they encountered about 30 Indonesians at this location on top of a jungle-covered hill. The lance corporal went forward with two men, but when they were only 10 yards from the machine gun, the sentry opened fire, whereupon the NCO rushed forward and killed him with a grenade. The enemy then opened fire on the small party, wounding the two men with the lance corporal. He made two journeys into the open and under heavy fire to drag his comrades to safety.

Looking into these slit trenches with scattered empty tins and ration packs, which were all Indonesian, it looked as if the action had happened only yesterday. We made our base camp near to this location, settled in and sent a three-man water patrol out to the river, where it would be fast flowing down by the border. McGurk, Thackeray and Miller set out with their rifles and to fill as many empty water bottles as they could carry.

They had been gone for only a short while when all of a sudden, shots rang out. It went silent and then came another burst of automatic fire. We all panicked. The platoon sergeant took a section of eight men along the track to find out what had happened. It turned out that McGurk had fired four or five rounds on two Indonesians who had panicked on seeing the patrol. McGurk was convinced that he had hit one of them. They did find the ground disturbed and traces of blood, but no sign of life. We were even more on the alert, but the automatic fire we had heard remained unexplained.

This was the end of the fourth day and the signals operator checked in by radio to the main camp 'Gunan Gadja' to report the incident. Usually we would have to throw the antenna far up into the trees and we could never reach the tops because these trees were a hundred feet high. We would throw a line with a weight on the end over one of the branches to the height of thirty feet and would get reasonable reception. Probably because we were on the wrong side of the border, we did have trouble getting into contact with base and moved position with the radio several times. It was standard procedure to radio the base every four hours and make a brief report.

Watching the Iban tracker cutting what looked like a dried up branch of a tree and chopping it in half with his perang long knife, we were amazed to see him holding it to his mouth and water come gushing out of it as if he were drinking out of a long wine glass. He then cut a large spiked fruit in half and began to eat the inside of it and from the look on his face it seemed to be very satisfying. Griff and I thought we would stick to our hard-tack biscuits, but they knew how to survive on what the jungle offered and what could and could not be eaten.

On the morning of the fifth day, the platoon commander decided he would send a section patrol from this position. Geordie Millar, Bob Griffiths and another five men, including myself, were sent out. We took the spare C41 radio. All three of us had had radio training and these patrols lasted about three hours. The requirement was that we reported back by radio every thirty minutes.

As the section of eight of us continued along the track and we were about three metres apart, we spotted movement! Then we heard automatic fire in front of us and we jumped for cover. It all went quiet and we waited a while before starting to crawl on elbows and knees alongside the track, with our armalites cradled in our elbow joints. Suddenly there was movement in the undergrowth and Geordie pounced. He lifted these two geezers together by the scruff of their necks, with his hands gripping them so tightly that their eyes nearly popped out of their heads. We made sure that there was no-one else about and as we turned round, there was Geordie with his rifle slung over his shoulder, dragging the two of them up the track by their shirts and with their feet dragging along the jungle floor towards the rest of the platoon. Then we heard, "Geordie's got them!"

There were only these two and when we realised they were not carrying weapons we concluded that they must have disposed of their arms to try and make us think that they were local village men. They must have had something to do with the disturbance earlier. We 'escorted' or more accurately 'dragged' them back to the RV (the patrol's base camp) and from there we made our way back up along the border. McGurk insisted that he had told us that he had seen someone. Mr Bond always said that it was better to be safe than sorry and I thought he talked sense.

The platoon sergeant and the commander interrogated the two prisoners with the help of the Iban tracker, because he could understand 'Indo'. We wanted to find out how they had disposed of their weapons but couldn't elicit any useful information. It would have been easy for them to throw them over the edge of the cliff and it would have taken a week for us to find them. So we never discovered where the machine gun fire we had heard earlier had come from. We then took the two Indonesians back to 'Gunan Gadja' base camp.

The prisoners would be interrogated further before being sent to Kuching and if it was proved that they were 'Indon's' or any other form of terrorist they would certainly be executed. It was now out of our hands. They were probably what we called 'Borneo Rebels' who were responsible for a lot of murders taking place. We were very shortly back in camp and were debriefed.

After debriefing, we were allowed the luxury of a shower! The only means of showering was to stand beneath a 45-gallon drum full of water. The toilets were unbelievable. There were six compartments covering a huge hole in the ground and with a piece of hessian as a doorway flap. The smell was terrible and there were thousands of mosquitoes buzzing about. It was, appropriately, named the 'Thunderbox'.

The following morning, it was my turn in the kitchen where my usual job of peeling potatoes for the entire company was waiting for me. A stove or oven had been dug into the ground (Imagine a pit dug into the ground about eight feet long, covered with cast iron grills and with 'jet burners' protruding from each end. They were a bit like the Atlas rocket motors and threw out a blue-white flame, three to four feet long.) On top of this wonderful contrivance were placed twenty-gallon dixies and not an automatic dishwasher in sight. It was a most unpleasant job because in addition to the hot sun, we had the heat from the cookers to put up with. This went on three times a day and after each meal, the dixies (extra-large saucepans) had to be scrubbed and the whole kitchen area cleaned also.

At about 18.00hrs, we would be allowed in the NAAFI for our ration of two cans of Tiger beer. Geordie would always manage to find a few more cans - usually by fair means. He would swap for cigarettes or chocolate and then he would be happy. At this point he would begin mimicking his own favourite singer, George Formby. His personal delight was 'Leaning on a Lamp Post' and he was perfect, playing his banjo and with the lads singing along. He was some character. Shorty Johnson would get some stick as he tried to get a couple more cans, which was a near impossibility. The Artillery section from the 105 Howitzers would be 'taking the piss' something rotten and shouting, "Come on Shorty! Be a sport!"

About eight thirty, the Orderly Officer would be on his rounds and telling us to clear the NAAFI and prepare for the blackout, which meant no lights whatsoever in the camp. The following day was going to be a hard one, so it was back to our camp beds and the rats and try to get some sleep. During the night, you would feel a sudden thump somewhere on your body and knew that it was probably a rat.

They were everywhere and none of them seemed to sleep at night. It was just something we had to get used to.

The next day we were due an air-drop of rations, ammunition for the mortars and howitzer shells. We blessed the RAF for our food, cigs, and beer - not forgetting letters and parcels from loved-ones at home. If it hadn't been for those aircrew, we would have had to truck and carry all of our stores by road and river, up and down mountains and through impossible jungle. We were totally cut-off from the outside world and totally relied on them and the squadrons of helicopters who ferried troops to and from the sites of major and minor incursions.

Some of those helicopter pilots were fantastic. They must have trained to fly up and down roller coasters because where they could position those monstrous machines were unbelievable. One incident comes to mind. There were three stranded SAS soldiers who were cut off from any outside help and called up the rescue helicopter. The pilot had found their position. The soldiers, despite their reputation for being able to get into or out of anywhere were unable to move, whilst being under enemy fire. The pilot flew his helicopter up river just below the tops of the trees with his rotor blade missing the trunks and branches by inches. He positioned the machine as close to the SAS men as possible. With the soldiers being waist deep in water, the winch man lowered the winch and hoisted the three soldiers into the relative safety of the open cargo area just below the pilot. The helicopter was unable to swing around and bullets were bouncing off the superstructure. The pilot had to reverse this huge machine out from a darkened forest, hovering only a few feet from the river. F/O Collinson received the DFC (Distinguished Flying Cross) for this heroic rescue and he will long be remembered for his flying skills.

Our platoon had been volunteered to supply the drop zone with a perimeter guard and the engineers had cleared an area the size of a football field. Bob Griffiths and I were escorted by our NCO i/c to the position where we would stay until the airdrop was over. Two hours earlier than the drop time, we would be placed in position to make sure it was safe. Once in position, we would camouflage ourselves and lie there for the best part of a day, listening to the screeching of the hornbills and parrots and watching the brightly-coloured birds of paradise and the thousands of multi-coloured butterflies - some of which were as big as a man's hand. It was like being in a Hollywood travel movie.

There was so much noise that sometimes I thought I was back in the steelworks, but we just continued to sit there 'camouflaged up' with 'cam cream' and buried in the undergrowth of the jungle. There were foraging ants about an inch in length and red in colour, which we called 'Ground Thieves'. If you dropped a biscuit, you could watch it walk away. If it was edible, these foraging ants would carry it off to feed their queen, the mother of the entire colony. About a million or so ants live in one of these colonies and when they go on the march, everybody moves out of the way.

Guarding the DZ

After we had been watching the ants for a while, an aircraft started its first approach, opening its gaping rear doors and pushing its cargo out whilst ensuring that the rigging lines did not become entangled. On one occasion, one of the crates that came out of a Beverley over-shot the DZ (Drop Zone) and a box of ammunition dropped 'late' of the drop zone. It landed on a bamboo long house inside the kampong, blowing its roof off. The next thing you saw was three people jumping from the building and running off with some speed. They were so lucky. The next thing that came over was a Belvedere helicopter with a landrover suspended from the under-belly. This was a godsend for the collection of the air-dropped stores.

A Beverley aircraft dropping rations over Gunin Gadja

Chapter 9

Guarding the 'Drop Zone. / The 'Lucky' Kampong / The Headman's 'Home Brew'/ Unloading the Drop Supplies

I was on duty with Bob Griffith and I always listened carefully to his advice and watched and learned from him. We had become quite good friends and he was telling me about his younger brother who had been posted to our company. He was put in '2 Platoon' and was twenty- two years old. I, on the other hand, was eighteen years, three months old. Bob was trying to get his younger brother into our platoon because he was very worried about him for some reason. As I recall, Bob was short and stocky, about twenty-eight years old and a really nice chap.

We were stuck there all day watching the parachutes falling from the side and rear doors of the Beverley aircraft. The lads who collected the rations had their work cut out in this heat. Every hour we had to report by radio. When we did, we were told that Pat McGurk had broken his arm on one of the crates - that was twice in about twelve months. He would have to be on light duties, so they would have to give him the job of batman to the company commander. I thought, "Rather him than me!" but he was the favourite for that job because he could manage it with one arm - not that he would be given any choice.

Bob and myself lay in our positions all day, watching for any movement in the jungle, until all the rations had been collected and transported up the steep hill on the men's backs. As they totally relied on us for their safety, we had to be extra-careful and alert. Bob told me that some of the lads were putting on a show in the NAAFI that night and it was '1 Platoon's turn.

We sat down and drew our two cans of Tiger beer and then the show started. All the lads started shouting, with the lads in drag and singing with Barella the centre of attraction, singing and cracking jokes. We had waited a month for this entertainment and it was well worth the wait.

Whilst the show was going on, only a few of us knew that Shorty Johnson hadn't finished unpacking the beer crates from the delivery, so Miller and one of the artillery section named Mulloy, decided to sneak into the rear of the NAAFI and pinch a couple of crates to keep the party going whilst Shorty was otherwise occupied. However, Miller and Mulloy got greedy and decided to go back for more. Unluckily for them, Shorty came back and caught them in the act and threatened to shoot them if they didn't clear out sharpish.

They complied with the order without hanging about, but unknown to Shorty they had already 'had him right over' for two crates of beer that we all enjoyed under candle light after the show. I didn't have much trouble getting to sleep that night as four cans of Tiger beer were enough to see me off.

The next day, we lay around in the hot sun, soaking up a few rays and watching the lads playing 'Three-Card-Brag' for cigs or, if it was a large pot in the middle, they would bet their cans of beer before they got them. That meant that someone would be happy or drunk that night. You could guarantee that Miller was involved in taking some of the winnings and hoping not to get caught. I didn't smoke at that time, but as a two-hundred carton of cigarettes cost virtually nothing, most of the lads took advantage. I watched the lads with these cigarettes lighting up and as soon as they lit it, they could take only two or three drags from it before the fag would fall apart because of the sweat running down their faces making the cigarette-paper wet and soggy. At this time, smoking didn't interest me. I was more concerned with keeping fit.

During that afternoon, a call came into the signals centre. A platoon that was out on a five-day patrol had radioed back to say that they had enemy contact and asked for covering fire. Within two minutes, the artillery section had their grid-reference and went into action. The artillery pounded the border area with 105mm shells all that day and the platoon returned the following morning. Fortunately, there had been no casualties. As we listened to the radio that night, we learned that there had been panic in Jakarta, with riots and looting, and consequent executions. All British and American civilians were trying to leave the country by the first available aircraft. Most of the population seemed to have taken to the streets and were demonstrating, trying to oust President Sukarno from power. As the Indonesian regular army was trying to bring things under control there, we were listening to reports of what was going on in Vietnam, just a couple of hundred miles away, across the South China Sea.

It was now the middle of January and the rest of the battalion were to join us from Kota Belud which was in the northern Borneo territory, near Jeseldon. They were due to join us in the next few days. I didn't know what to expect when they arrived. Roaring helicopter engines were arriving every ten to fifteen minutes with groups of twelve men. They were all men of the 1st Battalion the Durham Light Infantry and watching them leap with full equipment and rifles from the choppers as they hovered two or three feet off the ground, it was a sight to see. I couldn't explain the feeling of exhilaration to know that I was a part of all this. It was soon all over and everybody was settling in and meeting old mates.

Major Arnott giving a briefing

As I got to know some of the lads, I was amazed to find that they were all from the north east of England and the majority from Sunderland, Newcastle upon Tyne and Hartlepool. I knew quite a few of them from school and the steelworks where I was working before joining the army. One chap was Charlie Bassett who had left school the year before me. Ken Jackson and Stan Freak, the two tallest men in the company were both over 6'2". Ken had been sent to Singapore for treatment of 'jungle foot'. He had been 'No.1' on the GPMG and Tommy Griffiths was his replacement.

The next day we all had to be on the helipad for a company briefing by Major Jag Arnot. It was to remind us that we were on active service, that we must be alert and must keep our weapons with us at all times. We would be operating a patrol rota and each patrol would do one five-day patrol every third week. Just so that one group didn't have all the 'fun' all through January, we carried on with our patrols. We gradually got to know the rest of the lads and became familiar with the jungle terrain as we struggled on our patrols, with not very much happening until early February. Nothing could have prepared us for what was about to happen later that month.

A rumour went round that one of the patrols that had gone out on a 'Hearts and Minds'. Since an officer was not available, the patrol had been left to one of the senior NCOs. The second day out, they came upon a kampong where they made a bivouac and settled down for a little intelligence gathering - and what happened next was very intelligent.

Collecting stores after the drop

The headman was so pleased to see the British army that he got out the home-brew kit. Now, you know there's 'bought' home-brew and there's 'home' - brew. This was definitely a bit stronger than bought home brew. Up went the elbows and the brew started to disappear down the throats of the gathered party. As the party went on, it got a little over-excited. One of the patrol that had been left at the bivouac area to look after the tents and munitions was gathered into the throng. If anyone had come across this patrol, they would have thought that there was a battle going on inside the longhouse.

The longhouse was a simple affair - literally a long house, open-walled and with a thatched roof. There was a corral of wooden staves which was where the head man kept his pigs. Naturally, it became a little muddy and full of 'fertilizer' and when the revellers got a little 'bevvied up' they, of course, decided to throw one of their number into the pigsty. All names have been omitted from this little anecdote, you will notice, and no amount of bribery or liberal buying of pints will loosen my tongue. You know who you are….!

6th February 1966

We were expecting another air-drop and the DZ guards were already in position. I was asked to go gathering rations and ammunition. Usually eight men from each platoon were detailed to carry out this task. We were fully equipped with rifles

John Valentine and Terry Reaper prepare for DZ guard

over our shoulders and crowbars in our hands, and we would sit waiting for the aircraft to come over. The first wave of aircraft would be above us and these would be the Beverleys with the side and rear doors open. Large wooden crates would start to pile out of both sides of the aircraft and their parachutes would open almost immediately. When the large crates hit the ground, we could begin to collect them and roll up the chutes. Usually a couple of these would go missing because they made perfect trousers and tops. We found them very cool at night and named them 'Zoot Suits'. Next we had to return to the heavy lifting onto the back of a landrover (usually driven by Flicker Loveless, soon to be moved to an important position at Headquarters. His replacement was Totty Taylor) to transport the goods to the bottom of the hill and then towards the river which meandered around it.

Such goods as the landrover couldn't carry; we had to - on our backs. The first obstacle was the river and we placed a large tree trunk across it. It was about forty feet long and two feet wide, with handrails made of branches that you could hang onto. One mistake and you were in the water. It happened occasionally and the rations had to be recovered or you would be in trouble with the colour sergeant! We fixed a gantry across for heavier equipment such as artillery shells, but that was the easy part over!

Once across the river we had the steep climb of five hundred and thirty-nine steps. Each of us would make about fifteen trips up and down with these boxes on our backs and then we would hear the noise of another aircraft coming over - another

Alan leading 1 platoon up the 539 steps, carrying rations - each climb took half an hour. Ten trips up and ten trips down twice a day, was not unusual

Frank Branigan, signals operator

drop! They must be fuckin' joking! We had it all to do again and wouldn't get finished until late, probably about seven o'clock and hoping that the sergeant was in a good enough mood to open the NAAFI for our two cans of cold Tiger beer. The guards had been sitting there all day in full jungle greens and webbing in the hot sun. I bet they were glad to see the back of this day.

Barella, Noble and myself managed to sneak our cans back to our sleeping quarters - something that wasn't allowed - and also took a spare couple of cans to share between us as we tended to our sore backs. Next morning, there was a long line at the medical centre and the MO would give each man a codeine and tell him to soldier on. The odd few would be put on light duties such as peeling potatoes in the cookhouse under the portly gaze of Sgt Dempsey.

It was our turn to stay in camp this week and it would have been a lazy one but for the guard duties. We were told that Mr Bond was returning to the UK and we thought it a pity really because he was, for an officer, a really good bloke and well up on the rigours of jungle warfare. He would be relieved by a Lieutenant Deely, fresh from Sandhurst Officer Training School.

Terry Reaper outside the entrance to the rats' sleeping quarters. We slept under the corrugated roof above

Chapter 10

Rats and a Python / Top Brass Visit / Something Big Brewing / Second Airdrop / On Patrol with SAS in the Jungle

It was our night off after being in the NAAFI. We hadn't all been in residence together for a long time as there had always been one or even two of us on duty at the same time. I was reading a book under candle light with the two doors covered with hessian sacking to stop the light shining out. The orderly officer would be on the prowl and if he saw any light you would be in trouble.

As I lay there reading, I just happened to look up above the book and what I saw I could not believe. It was a fucking great snake! I whispered in a low voice, "Allen! Allen!" As the head of the reptile was coming towards me, I saw a machete (a jungle hacking knife) come flying across the room and it took the head of the snake clean off, just as I rolled out of its way. It turned out to be a python about seven feet long. It was a shame to kill it because these creatures did us the great favour of keeping the rat population down.

I don't think it meant me any harm, but I'm pleased that Allen didn't wait to find out. The bunkers beneath us were alive with rats and they would be jumping on the beds and everywhere you looked amongst the sandbags you would see a rat running from one hole to another, looking for a meal. I think I would rather put up with that than with the snakes. They terrified me and I don't think I got any more sleep that night just in case it had a mate. Next morning, everyone was having a laugh about my scare, but I knew that I would be a bit more vigilant in inspecting the sleeping quarters in future.

At this time, we knew that something big was about to happen. Helicopters were coming and going, with Major General Lea and some top brass, so it was obvious that some sort of action was being planned. Major General Hunt, Commander 17th Division Land Forces and a Major General Lea, Director of Land Forces in Borneo arrived, and we were warned to be at our best and on heightened alert at all times. We had to man all the gun and artillery positions on the base whilst they were with us. We were to be dressed in full 'jungle greens' and webbing with strictly no shorts, and that meant everybody, even Major Arnot.

Brian Banks manning an observation post

They stayed most of that day and that evening, the platoon commander told us that large groups of Indonesians had been seen crossing the border. A platoon of Australian light infantry had had a gun battle with them, suffering two killed and six wounded. The enemy Indonesians had suffered heavy casualties. The Australians came rather late into this conflict after the Rt. Hon. Dennis Healey of the British Government, convinced them that it was necessary to protect Malaya from Sukarno. We were warned to be more alert and to be ready for any attack or ambush, though it could be that they were just trying to put the fear of God into us.

Things changed from that day onwards. The sunbathing stopped and we were always found us something to do - repositioning the howitzers, correcting the firing of the automatic GPMGs on sustained fire, and strengthening the bunkers. We had to carry our own personal weapons with full magazine at all times and anyone caught not complying with this order was in real trouble. They even got us to build two more bunkers at each corner of the helipad, where we had to mount GPMGs instead of simply having the usual guards. They were really taking this threat seriously.

By the time we had been at it for three days, we told ourselves that we would be really delighted to go on a patrol instead of this hard graft. However, we knew that it was for our own protection in case we did come under attack. We realized also that this must be building up for a second airdrop to bring extra ammunition and rations because the threat was regarded as being serious. We could see the

105 howitzer at the ready outside the camp at Nibong

helicopters doing reconnaissance flights along the border. Signals traffic increased with constant radio messages in and out of the company commander's office.

That night we only had the NAAFI open for a very short time and then had to return to our sleeping quarters where we had a complete blackout. Next morning they posted guards on the helipad and the GPMGs were manned, as we were expecting more visitors. The helicopters started to arrive and altogether about thirty men disembarked. The majority were Ghurkas together with six soldiers from the SAS regiment. We were told that two SAS soldiers would accompany each platoon on all future patrols and that the Ghurkas would operate independently as a separate platoon.

My platoon ('1 Platoon') was chosen for the first patrol and told to be prepared to move at first light after our usual inspection and then to report to the helipad in 'sticks' of eight at a time. The rest of the platoon would lie in wait at the edge of the helipad under cover behind the sandbag bunkers. We were surprised to learn that we were being airlifted to a kampong near the border. Another three helicopters were hovering in the distance as the first landed and there was dust everywhere with the spinning of the rotor blades.

We ran towards the Wessex with all our equipment and with our heads down we struggled to get on board. Because everything had been done so quickly, the last two men had to sit in the doorway looking out with a Bren gun across their knees.

Border patrol

The flight lasted about fifteen minutes and as we went in to a piece of open ground near the first long house, we could see villagers running out of the way of the chopper and bits of debris flying all over the place from the speed of the rotor blades. We jumped out from the hatch and ran to the relative safety of the trees to cover for the rest of the platoon, which was still hovering above us in the remaining helicopters. After every one had landed, we re-grouped, ready to start our patrol and watched the four Wessex helicopters fly off into the distance. From now on, we knew it would be all legwork and as we left the village and wandered off into the jungle the whole population was watching and wondering what the hell was going on.

Patrolling in Borneo was always a strain as encounters with the enemy were a constant possibility, though when it happened, it was usually unplanned and unexpected. Whether we were the instigators or the victims of an ambush, contact with the enemy was often over in seconds. and the ability to shoot quickly and accurately was of paramount importance. It was a deadly game of cat and mouse, of bluff and counter-bluff and the patrol commander always faced the dilemma of walking a trail leading into an ambush or of treading on an anti-personnel mine. We had to hack our way through nearly-impossible secondary jungle at the rate of perhaps 200 metres an hour.

At 17.00hrs, it began to get dark and the patrols broke off the track to establish a bivouac for the night. This meant no smoking or brew-ups as movement in the jungle without light was impractical. A circular perimeter was established, sentries posted and a cold evening meal quietly eaten.

For most of the Borneo campaign, it was considered unsafe to cook in the jungle at night and we spent the 'silent hours' trying to get some sleep after our two hours on guard and with the rain belting down on us. I can't remember a single day or night without rain or some sort of storm and the only time we changed our clothes was when they were stinking, because they were permanently damp or even soaking. We sat there, very often shivering with the cold, hoping that morning would soon come when we could be on the move again to warm up. After standing and listening to all the strange noises of the jungle and the birds and animals coming to life, we would be more than ready to move very quickly when given the word.

We advanced, making a track by chopping our way through with our machetes and thinking to ourselves that we could have picked an easier route. We walked all day through rubber plantations, keenly on the alert and looking into these tall trees, which had little cups at their base to catch the white liquid that was running down the trunk. It was a perfect place for an ambush. All of a sudden, you would hear a loud crack like a shot and everyone would jump for cover because some stupid wanker had stood on a length of bamboo. It put the fear of God into everybody until we realised what had happened.

When we continued our advance, it would always be into yet thicker jungle, on the orders of the SAS as I don't think they liked the idea of open ground and this suited me fine in this war of nerves. They decided to take the hard way and shortly we would be wading through swamps, up to our waists in silt and mud with green moss floating on top. You cannot imagine the smell. We thought that everyone in the village we were approaching must have had a crap in this lot to feed the mosquitoes. There were thousands of them and we would be thankful to get out of this 'shite' and onto dry land.

After about an hour, we would be given about ten minutes to get all the leeches off our bodies. Now, one or two of the patrol would light a cigarette to burn them off. Usually we would pair-off to make sure that we got them from each other's backs before setting off again in our wet and stinking clothes. When we were at the base of the border, we set up camp just outside a village and after putting a perimeter around it, we went six metres outside and place flares on trip wires from tree to tree. It was time to get our ground sheets and ponchos out and to build our bivouac. Then maybe we could take our jungle boots off and change our socks and trousers that would be stiff with the dried mud from the swamps as if they had been starched.

Our feet would be red raw with rubbing against the inside of our boots, so one of us would make the bivouac while his mate made a quick change of socks, after filling them with foot powder. Two would be on guard at each end of the camp at all times - two hours on and four hours off. Just before last light you would see dozens of orang-outangs swinging through the trees and within a very short time it would be pitch black. Then all you could see were fireflies, hundreds of them, and everything would be silent.

Bob Noble with an Iban tracker on jungle patrol

Chapter 11

Noises in the Night / 'Trigger-Happy'/ River Crossings / Wading in Swamps again / Leeches on our Balls / Encounter with the Enemy / More River Crossing / 'Gunning Gadja' once more

When we got 'stand to' for thirty minutes the lads were a bit jumpy, because there were all kinds of noises that night and we had a few false alarms. About 02.00hrs, Bob Griffiths and myself were on guard and chatting away, trying to pass the time underneath the poncho that we had tied between the trees. We had the Bren gun's safety catch on 'fire' position and two spare magazines close by. I noticed Bob look around and I asked him, "What is it?" He told me to shut-up and listen - and then I heard it too - a kind of 'shush-shush' sound, together with a crackling of brush along the jungle track. It was getting louder as it came nearer to us. I heard Bob shout, "Shoot, you silly bugger!" because I was manning the Bren gun and it was so close we could see its eyes glaring at us, whatever it was. I wasn't going to wait to find out. I emptied a full magazine straight towards the track and was then quickly changing the magazine when Bob began firing his Armalite at what we thought must be Indonesians. We heard the loud crack of the trip wire going off but could see nothing. By this time, everybody was up and in their 'stand-to' positions. It was so silent you could hear a pin drop. That was the last sleep any of us would get that night because we were under constant 'stand-to'. Mr Bond told us to stay calm and alert but we never heard anything else that night. The next morning, we patrolled the perimeter and found a wild boar, and a right mess it was in too.

The lads had some fun calling us names and inferring that we were 'trigger-happy' but we wondered what they would have done in a similar situation. Within minutes we had moved out of this position, after breaking camp and packing our gear. We had nothing to eat, just a drink of water, because we would have given our position away to any enemy who happened to be in the area. We were quickly deep into the jungle surrounded by trees and came to a pass with cliffs towering over us on each side. They seemed to be made of granite or limestone and we deduced that there must be a waterfall nearby because of the roaring sound of rushing water. We had to get over this somehow, so we followed the river down to where the current slowed somewhat and we felt that it was safe to cross. The water was still very fast

Patrolling downstream

and the depth varied from waist high to shoulder height, so we crossed holding our rifles above our heads - happy to get rid of some of the stink that had been with us since wading in the swamp. I lingered as long as possible in the river, making out that I was keeping a lookout while the other lads crossed.

Anyone caught drinking the water would be put on a charge because all our drinking water had to be put through a personal water-purification kit. Leptospirosis (Weil's disease) is a fatal ailment caused by rat's urine and can kill in seconds. All you were allowed to do was to throw water over yourself and down the back of your neck to cool off - this being the only luxury permitted. Everyone got across safely and we were thankful, because this could sometimes be a hazardous task. On a previous patrol, Pte. Pete Slimmings from Hartlepool had lost his footing and was swept away by the fast-flowing water. Up to now he had been our solitary fatality in Borneo. He was buried in Ulu Pandan cemetery in Singapore with full military honours.

We climbed to the border in three stages because it was such a steep, hard climb. We had to keep stopping to burn the leeches off our bodies with a lighted cigarette-end. We were covered in them, even on our genitals. You try burning a leech off your balls with a lighted fag some time! Even now, the thought makes me cringe, but if you showed your feelings the lads would make a great joke out of it. If you just plucked the leeches off, their mouths would remain embedded in your flesh and septicaemia or gangrene would follow.

That river was the only laundry I knew of where you could get your clothes washed without taking them off and I felt an awful lot cleaner and better after standing in it. After taking my belt and ammunition pouches off my shoulders and buckling them back around my waist, we were on our way once again. In about fifteen minutes, I was completely dry in the hot sun. As we started going up the border, I just 'leaned into it' and mentally switched off my present predicament and thought about my family at home or being back in the steelworks' club, having a pint of beer - anything that would get my mind off this fucking mountain!

By late afternoon, we had reached the summit of the mountain range that separates Sarawak from Indonesia. Unknown to me, and some of the lads, the two SAS members had already broken off and left the patrol to go on one of their 'walk-abouts'. It was just two hours before last light and time to get a meal down us and a cup of tea or coffee, if we were lucky and the commander thought it safe to have a brew. It was about 16.00hrs and time to get in contact with base camp by radio. When we did manage to get through to them, our tea break was cut short because they ordered us to prepare to move and assist a platoon of 'B' Company who had encountered the enemy.

We moved very quickly but carefully along the border while we still had some daylight left. We were a long way from B Company, heading straight for their position, not by the usual tracks but navigating by map and compass, which made it more difficult and treacherous. By the time we neared their location, it was coming in dark and we could hardly see the man in front of us for the mist or fog. Being in constant radio contact with them, we could hear the occasional bursts of gunfire, as we drew closer.'7 Platoon' had no casualties thus far but they were pinned down and did not know the strength of the enemy. We decided to wait till first light before going any further because it was unlikely that they would attack at night and - if we were lucky - they might even simply pull out. As we spent the night just sitting and whispering to each other and sometimes nodding off, we were constantly awoken by the man nearest to us. If they weren't going to get any sleep, they were damn sure we wouldn't either.

It was fast approaching first light and as we 'stood to' we gradually began to see how they had come to be caught out as they had. On the Sarawak side of the border was a steep hill with trees and undergrowth, thick and undisturbed. We found it an impossible task to get through. There was only one way in and one way out, so we were told to split up into three sections and spread out, using the Indonesian side of the border where it was easier and safer to reach our target. It would have been suicide to simply stroll in there, especially when you couldn't see them, as they would be fully camouflaged or even hidden in the trees. If they remained perfectly still, it would be impossible to see them.

We got so close; I don't think they even knew we were there. It was nearly time for us to make some noise and make them realise that we were indeed there. We searched for a clearing in the canopy of trees and fired about six rounds from a 2-inch mortar. We knew where our blokes were and had a pretty good idea where they were. The only problem with this was that if the shells hit the tree tops, they would explode in a downwards fashion and anyone lying down or even positioned in the tree cover stood a more than good chance of being killed. If your mortar was positioned properly, you would rarely inflict wounds on your own troops - but there was always a possibility.

The trapped platoon was putting heavy machine gun fire towards the Indonesian side of the border and we heard screaming in between the firing bursts, so something must have done its job. The firing stopped and it was daylight. I don't know what anyone else was thinking, but I was terrified, staring into the jungle at every noise I heard.I would say, "What's that, Geordie?" and he would tell me to shut up as he was probably just as terrified as I was. All morning we just sat there, waiting and listening because it would have been foolish to move out of this position until we knew it was safe. We knew that the SAS were operating in this area too and that meant that we poor bastards would have to sit there all day.

The SAS would be trying to find and follow the enemy back to their main base. These men always operated in two or four-man patrols, and when they located the enemy's position, they would observe and report enemy troop movement, always at the risk of being seen or heard. If this happened, as it did on many occasions, they had their methods of escape. "Shoot and Scoot" they called it and it was every man for himself. We were always there for their support if they needed us, all day and all night and shivering because it got very cold at night. It was also very scary as we couldn't see the person next to us and all we could do was sit and wait till first light, which couldn't come soon enough as far as we were concerned. It was all because we had to wait for the two fucking idiots who were following the Indonesians to tell us it was 'all-clear' so we could get the hell out of there.

We were all hoping that the platoon commander didn't want to be a hero and continue to hang about after sitting and lying there for almost twenty-four hours. He didn't and we couldn't get out of there quickly enough and back down the Sarawak side of the border. After about two hours, we had to cross a wide river with cliffs on one side and trees on the other at the base of the border. The river was fast on this day due to the amount of rain during the night. Most of the time the water was shoulder-height and it was a real struggle to cross, but we all helped each other. The first man across tied a line from one side to the other and this was a great help. I don't think some of us would have got across without it to hang on to. It must have taken a couple of hours for us all to get over with each side of the river being covered at all times for security. This was the very same river we had crossed a few days before, but now it looked wider, faster and more dangerous. It was a great feeling to be back on dry land once again.

Shortly after this, we had to split up. '7 Platoon' went back to Pluman Mapu and my platoon back to Kampong Bunan Gega (nicknamed 'Gunning Gadja')

It was a great feeling to be back on the Sarawak side of the border with everyone safe and well, and relieved that all we had to do now was make our way back to base. It couldn't come soon enough. On our way back, we heard bursts of automatic gunfire - probably the Indonesians trying to put the 'shits' up us and doing a damn good job of it. There was no way of telling where the firing was coming from so we just ignored it, if it was in the distance and not go looking for trouble. As this just what the enemy wanted, we didn't take the bait.

A platoon of B Company, returning from patrol

'Our front room' in the camp at Gunin Gadja

Chapter 12

Fixing Accommodation / Patrolling with the SAS / Enemy Shelling / Enemy Night Attack / Setting out on a 7-Day Patrol

February 10th 1966

We were in the camp all week, making repairs and fixing up additional accommodation. Every constructed building in a forward base had to be dug into the hillside and protected with sandbagged walls, then these bunkers required to be covered with corrugated sheets to shield us from the rain otherwise they would flood out very quickly and become useless.

In turn, the sheets had also to be covered with sandbags to take the shine off them, because exposure to the sun can cause them to buckle and get so hot that you could fry eggs on them. Sandbags are excellent insulators and so another of their qualities is that they can deaden the sound of the deafening rain from the inside of the living quarters.

The hard work and ingenuity displayed in making these bases both secure and comfortable proved once again that Geordie is an expert at this kind of work. When the whole camp had been tidied up and a lot of paint used to make it more attractive looking, it wasn't exactly Butlins holiday camp, but it had certainly improved since our arrival.

February 12th 1966

We were about to set out on a three-day patrol along the border when once again we found that we were to have the pleasure of company. Two members of the Special Air Services (SAS) joined us. It wasn't very often that we had this honour and I was delighted when one of them found time to have a short conversation with me. He told me that he had originally joined the regiment after leaving the Marine Commandos and his mate had been in '1 Para'. Then they had both passed the SAS course. I didn't get his name and I think that he only spoke to me because I was the youngest and looked like a school kid, but I felt very privileged.

Ghurkas at Pluman Mapu

They didn't say much after that. Starting this patrol, it seemed that they always had a map in their hands and after scrutinising the hills and terrain, it was they who decided that we would take a route other than the old 'A1' track which took us round in a circle before going up the border. This time we would go straight up and we knew that this was going to be a hard test for our fitness and determination. We were led by our Iban tracker and lead scout, Thackeray, as usual. Half way up the border, it was difficult to keep our normal distance apart because we had to help each other up steep slopes and through the thick jungle.

As we climbed the mountain a few of the lads were getting into trouble because we were certainly no match for the SAS! These fellows have always done things the hard way and choose routes where they are least likely to be seen. It was no surprise then, when one of the lads collapsed with heat exhaustion and dehydration.

One of the SAS men took over the situation and gave the soldier salt tablets and tried to calm him down. Eventually, they said it was time to get on the radio and call in a helicopter to get him out, because he wouldn't be able to continue with the rest of the patrol. Even if he continued, he would slow us down too much and possibly get someone killed. What these men wanted they got and even the platoon commander had no say in the matter.

We found a small clearing and started chopping the trees and bushes so that the helicopter could land. It was the afternoon of the 13th February and we could see the chopper circling above us. They had sent a Wessex helicopter, which could carry eight to twelve passengers of normal weight together with equipment. As it hovered above us, we struggled to get the soldier into a sort of chair that was attached to the winch rope hanging down from the side of the chopper. Eventually, it took off with its cargo and we were all told to get our kit on and get moving again in case the enemy had seen the helicopter land or had even heard it.

We moved quickly away from that location, moving even faster than ever before, chopping our way through the undergrowth or sometimes pushing it to one side. We could tell that no-one had set foot on this ground for a very long time because there were no tracks, just thick jungle. Late that afternoon we reached the top of the border, walking at a steady pace and every ten or fifteen metres casually lifting our eyes from the ground to scan the trees above, looking for any movement in case of an ambush. As I turned, I could see the rest of my mates kneeling down on one knee with their armalites to their shoulders. Their eyes were wide open and their faces blacked out with camouflage cream. Nobody made the slightest sound and all communication was done by hand-signals to each other. It was so silent you could hear a pin drop.

It was late afternoon when we reached the RV. and as we arrived, the SAS prepared to move out. They stood there with their Bergens (special SAS backpacks) on, 'cam.cream' on their faces and wearing bush hats and they simply wandered off into the jungle with an armalite cradled in their arms as if they were going on a Sunday afternoon stroll. These men would patrol the nine hundred mile jungle border between Indonesian territory and that of the British Dependents. This was just one of the many patrols they had done and it wouldn't be the last. They were, in all probability, already on their way to another secret operation.

On the way back, we could hear the sound of shelling coming from 'A' Company area. The Indonesians must have watched us moving out of the camp and consequently knew it was under-strength. The crafty bastards were shelling the far end of the camp where a platoon of the South Wales Border Regiment were positioned. The Indonesians must have dropped some fifty mortar shells, but luckily, the Welsh got off lightly with no reported casualties and not even sight of the enemy. However, as the Indonesians made their escape back to the border, the Ghurkas had a little surprise set up for them and later reported that four of the enemy had been killed. When we arrived back in camp, we were told to go to our 'stand to' positions and man the machine guns around the perimeter in case we were attacked a second time. We were on constant 'red alert' for the next two days - evidently 'No Rest for the Wicked'!

Things seemed to have calmed down and over the next few days we gradually got back to the normal routine of '2 hours on - 4 hours off' guard duties. When it was my turn for guard duty, I was positioned at 'No. 1 Post' which had the usual sandbagged walls and corrugated tin roof with further sandbags on top. A GPMG machinegun on 'Sustained Fire' role was mounted on a fixed tripod with a constant feed of hundreds of rounds from a brown munition box. Within arm's reach in front of me was a control panel which would operate the trip-flares and claymore mines. These ingenious devices were not meant to be trodden on, but were mounted on a tripod and pointed towards where you thought the enemy might be coming from. They could be fired by various means, either trip-wires, electrically or manually. They had a safety fuse and a 'Thirty-Three Detonator Electric Dynamo Condensor (EDC)' and consisted of a high-explosive charge directing 4,000 to 5,000 steel ball bearings at a 45 degree angle. If set correctly, they provided a very effective 'Kill Area'.

Miller and myself were on guard duty from 22.00 till 00.00 and had to be silent with no smoking as the commander's sleeping quarters were directly underneath where you were standing. At about 23.30, we were scanning to the front of us and whispering to each other that we had heard something when at that very minute the guard commander walked in and we reported what we had heard. He stayed with me and sent Miller to awaken the platoon commander Mr Bond, who in turn turned out the whole company.

We had been 'aware' for some time now and were 'stood to' just listening when at about 03.30 the shock came! One of the enemy had walked through a trip-wire, tripping a flare as he did so and it was fired high into the air, lighting up all the jungle in front of us. You could see as far back as the river downhill. When we saw three or four figures running between the barbed wire we opened up almost immediately with the GPMG machine gun. By this time Major Arnot was in the observation post and we set off another two flares, manually because we expected that an attack would almost certainly come. When it did not, it was obvious to us that the enemy were trying to break down our morale with hit-and-run tactics.

We waited until first light and Mr Bond organised a perimeter patrol of platoon strength to patrol the outer fence. As it was such a large hill, we would descend half-way down the famous 'Five Hundred and Thirty-nine Steps' and then cut off into the thick jungle to circle the hillside so as to be clear of claymore mines and other booby traps that we had laid in the past. To walk in this terrain we had to lean at a forty-five degree angle, because the hill was so steep and it was so very easy to lose your footing. The brush in front of us was mainly bamboo and difficult to cut. We found empty ration tins and used shell cases everywhere which had been used in some earlier attack on the camp, but there were no Indonesians. They had just disappeared into the jungle, leaving no other trace. We did not return for another three or four hours, but found no enemy activity anywhere in the vicinity.

Our section spent the rest of the day arming the '36' grenades - three boxes of them and sharing them out between the platoons. Then we stripped down the Bren guns and the GPMG. We used quite a few rolls of '4 by 2' cloth to clean our weapons that day. The sergeant placed two 2 inch Mortars on the floor and a signalling pistol with a 2 inch diameter barrel for us to clean as well, because we might well need them. As it turned out, we did need them on more than one occasion. They proved to be a great asset and well worth the trouble of carrying the extra weight. Because of all this cleaning and preparing, there was a lot of talk amongst the lads that we must be getting ready for an all-out invasion of Indonesia.

18th February 1966

All the company were instructed to report to the helipad for a briefing by the company commander, Major Arnot. He told us that we were going on seven-day patrol between Sarawak and the Kalimantan jungle border, but what he failed to tell us was that we would be penetrating ten to fifteen thousand metres into Indonesian territory. Such operations, when it is considered most likely that there would be contact with the enemy, are coded 'Claret' operations. These enemy would be either Chinese border terrorists, trained by the Indonesians or regular troops. In either case, they were well-trained and well-led. Our two SAS friends had reported enemy activity close to the border region at a settlement called Luboc Saba, but what we did not know at that time was that it lay on the Indonesian side of the border.

On patrol in the jungle

Chapter 13

Seven Days Rations & Into the Jungle / Lousy Wet Nights / The Helipad Booby-trapped / Lenny March and the Ants / '8 Alma' Lays Down a Barrage

The next morning, we reported to the cookhouse area at first light dressed in full jungle greens for our last meal before leaving, as we would be moving out shortly afterwards. We made sure to have a light meal in case we suffered later that day. Then we drew seven days' rations and also extra ammunition. Each man carried a bandolier of two hundred rounds of '7.62' for the Bren guns and two '36'hand grenades each. Shared out between the platoons were four claymore mines with '33' electric detonators' and a 2 inch Mortar which each platoon would carry in turn, sharing out the load between them. There were, of course, other important things such as malaria and salt tablets together with mosquito repellent to stop the little fiends biting us.

Dog tags are identity discs worn around the neck with name, rank, service number and blood group stamped on them. These are compulsory on active service but we were given a roll of black masking tape to bind them together and cover them so that they wouldn't shine or rattle together. So we set off, loaded up like pack mules. This was to be no ordinary patrol. It would be the real thing and we were going straight into it. '2 Platoon' led by two hours then came '1 Platoon' followed by '3 Platoon'. The route taken was the old 'A1', the jungle path we had taken on many occasions on our way to the border.

On the way we had to go through three Kampongs (the villages on sticks), which were not all deserted - though riddled with exotic diseases. Usually we would stop to see if we could help with our advanced medical supplies, but this time we couldn't, as this was a very important operation and we could not afford any delays. We were led by Lieutenant Deely, a 'freshman' from Sandhurst who was taking over from Mr Bond, now on his last patrol before returning to the UK. Lt Deely was to be our new platoon commander. He was quite tall, of slight build and spoke with a refined accent. He was very young and didn't have much experience in jungle warfare, though he had a good reputation for map reading, so we had little chance of getting lost. We were all sure that Major Arnot would be keeping an eye on him and the platoon sergeant Charlton. '2 Platoon' commander was Lt. Kirk with Cpl. Bartlett as section commander. '3 Platoon' was led by Lt. Harris and Sgt. Sherlock. Major Arnot was in overall control of the operation and was in constant radio contact as we headed towards the border.

We were always being told to be on the lookout for mines and booby traps because the enemy usually placed these traps where they would be least expected. Despite the warnings, one member of '3 Platoon' stood on a 'Punjee Stick' (a sharpened bamboo spike) and it penetrated his leg. He had to be taken out by chopper and to Bali Ringing field medical centre by helicopter.

At the end of the first day, our platoon was at the base of the border and '2 Platoon' was near the top. '3 Platoon' had taken another route. We were told to make camp, so out came the ponchos and ground sheets and we made our beds for the night - the first of many nights.

Griffiths and I made our bivouac and then out came the mess tins and hexagon burners for a brew up and a meal of beef block and curry powder to see us through till morning. Miller, Noble and Sgt. Charleton had marked out the perimeter and sited the Bren gun at a good observation point and we were paired off for guard duty. It was to be 'two hours on and four off ' until midnight when it was the turn of Geordie Miller and me to relieve Barella and Noble. Just our luck! The rain started - of the monsoon type - and we got drenched, so that meant that we would be wet, shivering and cold all night with very little sleep. The noise from the rain like golf balls hitting the tops of the trees was deafening, which meant that we had to rely on seeing the enemy if they came, because you for sure you wouldn't hear them.

Wrapped in our ground sheets, we didn't see the point in wakening our relief, but we did so, just in case they said we had fallen asleep on duty, and that would be a guaranteed fifty-six days minimum jail sentence. If the enemy did come along and find us off guard and asleep, it would mean certain death.

Next morning at first light, we 'stood to' for 30 minutes and as we did so, we could hear the howitzer shells pounding the border where it was known to be a terrorist route. Probably the SAS would be directing fire onto these targets. Then we broke camp and began making our way up the border, climbing up five paces and sliding back down two, and holding onto branches to pull ourselves up as the rain belted down and made it yet more slippery. The rain would stop as suddenly as it had started. It was one damn struggle to get to the top and we were sure that Major Arnot had given us the 'best' route - a joke, of course! We reached the summit of the border at midday on the 19th February and by this time '2 Platoon' were well into the Kalimantan jungle of Indonesia with '3 Platoon' close behind. We were ordered to proceed along the border to a helipad as the C/O was to give us a visit later that day.

We arrived at the helipad only to find that it had been mined and booby-trapped. One thing was sure, the C/O would not be coming that day, at least not until the helipad had been cleared, and that would take quite a while. We were told to dig in and hold position on top of the border, which was about ten metres wide - on one side Sarawak and on the other side Indonesia.

We stayed at the helipad and cleared the mines and booby traps, a task that took all that day. We made our camp for the night and were lucky in so far as we got to use our sleeping bags, because it was so damn cold at this high altitude that we would be shivering even so. We only needed two guards at either end of the camp that night, as the sides were too steep to climb. We usually had a piece of string (usually Para cord) tied from each bivouac to the guard posts, because it was so dark that you couldn't see the man in front of you. The only way to find your way from the guard posts to your sleeping quarters was by following this piece of string. This Para cord would continue around each side of the camp to make sure that nobody fell over the edge. The canopy of the treetops was so thick that you couldn't see a fucking thing and because sound travelled so far at night, every word had to be whispered.

It wasn't easy to get some sleep because the night air was so cold that you would be shivering in your jungle greens even inside a sleeping bag. If these bags happened to get wet, they would weigh two stones. With luck, we might be able to turn them inside out and hang them on a tree to dry and just hope that they would be dry before setting off again. If this proved not to be possible, we would be carrying extra weight for the rest of the day.

In the morning, it started to break daylight about 06.00 and we were damn glad to see it.We were all waiting in our positions for first light, lying on our stomachs, with our weapons at the ready and safety catches on 'automatic'. For those lucky ones who had managed to get some sleep, it was a fresh start. For those who hadn't, this day would be one hell of a struggle because it would never really get very light in the thick jungle. We were just glad to see some sort of daylight, because these fucking Indonesians didn't care whether it was day or night, they would still attack. It was their country after all.

Another day was going by without incident and we were all getting a bit fed up with the ants and mosquitoes. Then the platoon commander decided it was safe to have a brew up, providing it was all done from inside one of the slip trenches. One man would be responsible for the tea and passed it around in turn as he made each cup. We sat there, drinking out of our aluminium cups that burnt our lips and watching Lenny March cutting the branches of a tree to make a lean-to. These consisted of three sticks arranged at an angle and with tropical leaves laid against them. Since we were guaranteed rain almost every day or night, these little shelters proved very effective in keeping you dry.

Lenny carried on working with his shirt off when, suddenly somehow, an ants nest fell on him! You never saw anybody move so quickly - they were down his pants

Howitzer at the ready at Gunin Gadja

and he was covered from head to foot in these red ants. Running about like a headless chicken, he gabbed the mosquito repellent and squirted it down his pants. When he did, he realised the pain he was going through. It wasn't the ants but the repellent - concentrated, it burns like hell! By the time he had got them all off, he looked as if he had been lying in the sun for a week. with no clothes on. Anyway, we all had a good laugh out of it, though Lenny didn't see the funny side of it. The bloody ants had really made a meal of him - when he had to put his shirt and webbing back on, it brought tears to his eyes for the rest of the day, whilst we continued to take the piss out of him.

February 20th 1966

After spending another dark and miserable wet night on the border, we started the day by 'standing to' and listening to the shells pounding the positions over the border from our base camp. By this time we were getting used to the shells, and the previous night we had been able to set our G10 watches for the commencement of the barrage. When the guns came into action, it meant that it must be '8 Alma' Commando Light Battery Royal Artillery (more commonly known as 'Lord Alma's Black 8 Commando Battery'). They were stationed at our base camp and always gave us excellent support with their two 105mm Howitzers, being constantly ready to bring down fire at a moment's notice.

Lord Alma's real name was Major George Atkins and he gave the gunners advice whilst counting the shells as they exploded, hoping that he would be able to think up convincing reasons for their expenditure. He also had under his control two 4.2 inch Calibre Mortars which were attached to one of our bases - one of the platoon commander's little secrets! A Lt. Middlemass was in charge of the Artillery Section and Sgt.Chris Batty was in charge of the howitzer.

When it was first light, we were told to pack our kit and prepare to move. We did so without so much as a cup of tea, but only a sip of water. As we were getting deeper into the jungle on the Indonesian side of the border, we had to chop our way through the thick undergrowth, taking well over two hours to cover four or five hundred metres. I thought I felt something on my feet - it was a fucking snake. I bet it was six feet long. It had started to wrap itself around my ankle, but changed its mind and was gone as fast as it came, but it really shook me up. It was bad enough to have to put up with the lizards and the ants, but snakes! That's when I realised that most of the platoons were going through similar experiences.

Emergency evacuation from the Borneo / Indonesian border

Chapter 14

Iban Trackers Desert / An Ambush is Prepared / Four Days Lying in the Rain

It was time to report to company HQ. by radio and to contact '2' and '3' platoons and say that everything was 'OK' at this time. We had orders to proceed further down the Indonesian side of the border, but this is where we had another problem - the Iban trackers were complaining that they wanted to be issued with an SLR instead of their usual Remington shotguns. The platoon commander asked Major Arnot over the radio and he refused, as '2' and '3' platoons were having the same problem with their trackers and interpreters. Because they knew that they were on the Indonesian side of the border and were in danger, they were also asking for more money. They were normally paid in cash at the base camp. Both requests were refused.

At this point we were told to check all our equipment and ammunition and to get a drink of water and a cold meal down us - just biscuits or oatmeal as it would be our last for nearly a week. Unknown to us at the time, we would have to leave our packs and rations at a clearing we came to and conceal them in the thick undergrowth. For the next few days, we would have to survive on 'hard tack' ie: biscuits and chocolate - only what we could carry in our side pouches and pockets. There would be strictly no brew-ups as you could smell the 'Hexagon Burners' half a mile away and this would be a dead give-away to any enemy in the area.

We went further down the border into Indonesia. It was all downhill and we had to stop every few minutes to make sure that we weren't running into an ambush. To make certain, the lead scout would advance forward and we would wait till he signalled back to us to say it was 'OK' to continue. It was slow, but sure. It was getting late and time to lie low because nothing moves in the jungle at night, and we knew that the enemy would have listening posts out in the least-expected places and would hear any sound.

We sat there all night, wrapped in our ground sheets because if you didn't, you would wake up and think you were having a cold bath - that's how bad these tropical storms would get. You could see the lightening bouncing off the tops of the trees - a nice sight, but a frightening one. We could sit reasonably

L/Cpl. Sid Pugh briefing 2 Platoon

comfortably on the stump of one of these huge trees as the rain hammered onto the ground and listen to it rushing past in a never-ending river running down the border. You would sit there all night sometimes in two or three inches of water and changing position every five minutes to try and get comfortable as the rain ran off our bush hats and down our necks. It was an 'Act of God' and we had to put up with it.

The next morning, after the usual 'standing to' and listening to the crack and bang of the shells landing over the border, we were on the move again. We had our orders to proceed further into Indonesia and position ourselves 300 metres behind '2 Platoon' and that is what we did - not knowing that we were going to sit there for another three days. I was alongside Bob Griffiths and had the odd laugh and joke with Miller, Noble and Allen Barella who were not too far way from us. We would say anything to pass the time more quickly. Just sitting, listening and looking into the jungle was like watching a nature-study programme. You would see every insect and reptile in the jungle - centipedes, millipedes, ants - You name it and we had seen it. Almost half the bastards bite and the other half are simply poisonous.

On the 21st February, '3 Platoon' came across an old Indonesian gun position constructed of bamboo, while on patrol. There was evidence that it had been used recently, judging by the empty tins that were lying about the area. A few hundred metres directly behind that was a kampong. Lt. Harris and Sgt. Sherlock together

Tommy Griffiths caring for Alan Barella's dog while Alan was on patrol

with an interpreter and the lead scout Dougy Elliot, went to talk to the headman. He wasn't very happy and was complaining about the shells that were being fired from our base camp, saying that they had wiped out his village called Lubok Sabot. He said that luckily, he had managed to evacuate after the second shell landed. Anyway, we managed to calm him down with bribes. He wanted to show us the damage the shells had done, but Lt. Harris refused to go with him, as he knew that this was no accident. It was a target that the SAS had reported as having had enemy activity in the village the previous day.

At this time, 1 Platoon were Rear Protection about three hundred metres behind 2 Platoon, who were lying at the side of the track on high ground overlooking the track. We heard a lot of gunfire and some explosions that afternoon. It sounded as though it was only a couple of hundred metres from our position. We were told to stay where we were as it was 3 Platoon who were making all the noise and they had the situation under control. We were also told that there was a force of at least sixty Indonesians troops in the area that day.

By this time we knew Major Arnot's plan was to draw the enemy into the ambush that we had set for them. We heard that all was well so we laid low and 3 Platoon stayed where they were on the track leading to the gun position. It was another cold and quiet night. I don't think anyone got any sleep after that. We were given pills to keep us awake - I don't know what they were. We just swallowed the damn things and they did help alleviate some of the misery.

Bob Noble and Alan Barella

22nd February

It was on this morning, at 08.00hrs, that word came back to us that 3 Platoon had set fire to an Indonesian stronghold 2,000 metres inside enemy territory. This being the gun position they had visited the previous day, they had thrown phosphorous grenades and fired some three hundred rounds of ammunition when they found it occupied by a small force of Indonesians. After engaging the enemy, some of whom were overpowered and the rest of whom fled, 3 Platoon then set fire to the gun position. They were told to make plenty of smoke whilst doing so and they certainly did that before moving back towards the border.

Major Arnot then decided to put an ambush into effect. The platoon commanders were having a right old row with the Iban trackers who were still complaining and threatening to leave us if their demands were not met. After they heard the gunfire, they said they had had enough and the six trackers and interpreters left us. We were amazed and made sure that they headed back towards the border. As they knew that there were Indonesians close by, they were determined that they weren't going to be caught up in any conflict and possibly injured or killed.

Whilst all this was going on, the lads had positioned two claymore mines on the track which would be aimed in the direction from which they thought the enemy would approach, and which would be set off electrically by the first 'cut-off'

Observing enemy movements in the border

group. If they came to investigate what had gone on, we had organised a little reception party for them. We had, of course, no idea we were going to be out in the jungle for at least another week, nor what lay ahead of us. Equally, we had no clue as to what Major Arnot had planned if the ambush was sprung.

He deployed his three platoons very carefully along and overlooking the river to the front. Having the safety of his troops foremost in his mind, we were told that 2 Platoon was to be in front at the ambush position as the main 'killing group'. 1 platoon was positioned as Rear Protection and 3 Platoon to the right of 2 Platoon, which was 300 metres up the steep slope on the main track towards the border. Our Platoon was positioned in a circular formation and every angle was covered by a Bren gun placed at each end where the track started and finished.

We were ordered to camouflage-up and remain in our position, so we did what we were told and waited and waited and waited. It was so silent. The quiet was undisturbed except for the orang-outangs, swinging in the tree-tops, completely unaware of the groups of armed men a hundred feet below them, disguised as new mounds of earth. It was as if we were not even there and the ants and mosquitoes had a field day biting us. We stayed in that position for another four days with only biscuits, chocolate and the occasional sip of water. By this time, we were filthy and unshaven and the maggots and insects were crawling on our clothes and bodies. Even so, some managed a small laugh and joke.

Left - right: Lance Cpl. Patterson, little Geordie Ray and Bob Noble

By this time, Garroway was ticking like a fucking clock - in simple words, he was shitting himself, as usual. Mind you, he wasn't the only one. We were all in the same boat, you might say and a bit pissed-off. We thought we should have been back at the base camp before now instead of wasting our time in this position, with cramp in our legs. If we moved, we were told to keep still.

Our clothes were soaking wet - if we could have changed them it would not have been so bad, but we couldn't and they had to dry on our bodies. They were always damp or wet, so that pulling our shirts from our skin was a relief, but the jungle greens were so thin that we would be shivering from the cold. If we got the chance, we would take our jungle boots off for a minute to wring our socks out and our poor feet would look like lumps of tripe, all white and shrivelled up. We would try to get the circulation going again before putting our wet socks back on - our spare ones were in our packs at the RV. We had a struggle to put our boots back on swollen feet and lacing those boots from your foot to just below your knee took a long time. We had to be quick so as not to get caught with our boots off.

24th February 1966.

It was about 8.30 in the morning and we were still in the position we had held for the past couple of days. At first light, a section of 3 Platoon was ordered to move from their position and patrol the perimeter following reports that someone had heard noises. They would do the patrol and take up their original 'ambush position' to the right of 2 Platoon alongside the river. To get around the perimeter, they had to come through our area and as they approached, we could see that though they were very tired, wet and unshaven, they could still have the odd laugh and joke amongst themselves. The odd one would say, "We're wasting our fucking time here!"

First to come through was our lead scout, whose name was Doug Elliot. It was up to him now that the Iban trackers had deserted us. He was one of the lads from the pits (Blackhall Colliery, which is close to my home town of Hartlepool). Next came Lt.Harris whom we had nicknamed 'Jet Harris' because he looked like the guitarist from the 'The Shadows' though, of course, we didn't use this 'handle' within his earshot! After about fifteen minutes came the last two men bringing up the rear, the Lawton brothers, who were always together. The job of the last man was always to make sure that we weren't being followed by the enemy and they would be as careful as the lead men. By the time they had all gone through we had over ninety men in position at the ambush site as rear protection, and we were all wondering how long this was going to go on for.

We just sat and waited.

Ration drops by a Wessex

Chapter 15

Days Spent Lying in Ambush / Going out after Water / Warning that Enemy Troops are Approaching / Battle Commences/ Thomas Griffiths is Killed / Casualties Flown Out

About midday, we heard a radio message informing us that two persons, unarmed, had walked straight into the ambush area. Three men from 3 Platoon were told to surprise them and take them prisoner. They bound and gagged them after a quick interrogation and put them under close arrest. Later, we found out on the radio that they were Indonesian village men who had been checking traps they had set for animals that they could use for food. If we had simply let them go, they could have given us away to any enemy that was in the area and we weren't prepared to take that chance. They had to remain with us until the end of the operation.

Sometime during that day they were sending a Wessex helicopter in with supplies and extra rations. They would make the drop and be out of there as quickly as possible, and you can be sure the lads were looking forward to this. From where I was lying I could hear the sound of rotor blades for about five minutes, then all went silent. Such extra rations that did come, I personally didn't see much of. The rest of the day passed quietly away. We were running out of drinking water but were told to keep away from the river that was close by. The platoon commander told us to keep away in case an Indonesian patrol boat came along and saw us, thus giving the game away. He instructed us to go up the border and find a stream that would be clear and fit for drinking.

Our section was told to take as many canteens and water bags as we could carry and fill them. When we got to the stream that ran down the border, it was about six hundred metres from our position and uphill all the way. This time, we travelled light. All we took was an Armalite Automatic, otherwise known as an 'M15' with three magazines of 18 rounds each. Safety catches were on 'automatic' at all times and the water bottles were strapped around our waists. We knew that it would take about two hours to get to the stream because of the hard climb that lay before us. We were the lucky eight, because when we got to the stream we could put two men on guard while the rest of us filled the water bags and were able to have a wash and freshen up. The other lads weren't so lucky - they hadn't had a wash for five or six days and missed this chance too.

We had two water-bags per couple to carry after putting sterilising tablets in and straining the water so that it would be fit for drinking by the time we got back to the position. The water bags were a lot like plastic shopping bags - a length of branch would go through the handles and then they would be suspended between two men's shoulders. We carried these all the way back to the ambush position and when we arrived back at last light, we shared the water out between the platoons. The lads were very grateful that they had got a drink at last, and then it was back to sitting and waiting.

26th February.

At first light in the morning, we were told to prepare to pull out at 09.00hrs. Having sat there for the last week for nothing, you could see that the lads were really pleased as the odd smile lit up their faces and they thought of being in the NAAFI with a couple of cans that night. We had 'stood to' that morning, wondering if the company commander had given the base camp another grid reference for the artillery shells. We remembered the village that had been destroyed over the past week and didn't want innocent people to be killed.

At 08.00hrs, we were preparing to pull out when a message came over the radio that a force of enemy troops was advancing along the track! On our side of the river near '2 Platoon' and on either side of the fast-flowing water was an embankment and we could see the enemy below us. They were about thirty to forty in strength and looked really smart with their blue helmets. They were walking straight into the ambush. It was 08.30hrs and the first thing Griffiths and I heard was a huge explosion. It was the claymores and at least four of the enemy had been killed and about six others wounded.

Then we heard the Bren guns open up at the cut-off groups. It was non-stop and the fire power was unbelievable. The enemy reacted immediately. Turning in their tracks and running with their weapons at 'high port' firing short bursts, they were led by their platoon commander who stood out a mile with his rank shoulder lapels, bright blue helmet and pistol as he waved them on, encouraging them to attack us. We thought they were all fucking mad men, ducking and diving between the trees as they charged uphill. Tommy Griffiths stood up to get a more accurate shot at the officer who was charging towards him. Griffiths took aim with his M15 Armalite and emptied the full magazine into the Indonesian's face. The deadly spray of bullets from the machine gun cut his head completely off his shoulders - not so much a decapitation, more a total destruction.

The enemy fell unusually silent for a few seconds until the realisation that their officer had been killed had sunk in. Then the orders rattled out and they started putting in heavy mortar fire on 2 Platoon's position within a few seconds of the ambush being sprung. We heard a voice heightened with a little panic come over

Howitzers in action on 26th Feb. 1966

the radio, asking for support for 1 Platoon and our platoon commander ordered that we drop everything but our weapons and ammunition and move as quickly and in as orderly a fashion as possible down the hill towards our besieged comrades at the river's edge. Bearing in mind that it had been raining heavily, it seemed that a cascade of well-armed bodies was sliding and running down the steep hill as we grabbed at anything that would stop our fall from becoming injurious.

At the moment we were on the move, and running towards their position, the whole jungle seemed to come alive with mortar and machine gun fire. Bullets and shrapnel were flying everywhere and you could hear it ricocheting off the trees with cut branches falling from above. The fire power was intense and it seemed that everything was happening in split seconds. It was confirmed that we had one man dead and two wounded. We came upon a small clearing, which was rare in this jungle, and stopped to hold position and receive a radio message from our '514 Signals Troop' radio operators. We were told that 2 Platoon had pulled out of the ambush position so we immediately went into an all-round defensive position covering the all-round area. We waited as 2 Platoon, who were about 200 metres away from us and withdrawing fast, headed straight for us. The enemy were, by this time, close behind them and raining mortar fire down on them from two positions. At this point, the major requested artillery support from our base camp.

Bob Griffiths and myself were stood behind a tree, trying to protect ourselves from shrapnel and Barella and Noble were close by. The platoon sergeant approached us virtually on his hands and knees, as he was such a tall man - well over six feet when he stood up. He spoke to Griffiths, who was kneeling beside me and informed him that it was his brother Thomas who had been killed. At the time it happened, Cpl. Bartlett and Lance Cpl. Finn had pulled him clear and there was nothing they could do to help him as he had been killed instantly by a bullet through the heart. The company medical officer, Bob Hall, had done what he could, but it was hopeless.

Bob Griffiths just sat there for a few minutes in shock. We could see some of our blokes running towards us with a stretcher and a body on it wrapped in a poncho, with Major Arnot helping one of the wounded. That's when Bob realised that it was his brother on the stretcher. I looked at Bob and suddenly he threw his webbing to the ground and ran towards the enemy with an 'M15 Armalite' machine gun blazing away, emptying a full magazine towards the oncoming Indonesians until Noble and Barella ran to assist him, calm him down and pull him out of there. At that moment, I saw Pte Hope, who was wounded with a huge gash in his back from his shoulder to his waist. The blood was pouring out of him like a fountain and half his back seemed to be hanging out. As I tried to assist him we couldn't believe that he had just come out of the ambush and was still on his feet and walking with the blood running down his trousers. He was still insisting that he could carry on as the lads made him lie on the floor and took his webbing off together with his shirt - what was left of it. The wounds were too severe for the lads to handle so the platoon medic, Bob Hall, took over with morphine and field dressings to dull the pain and get the bleeding under control.

Bob Hall certainly knew what he was doing and remained calm under fire with Keith Hope trying to get to his feet and persistently trying to walk out of there, which he did for quite a while. I could see Cpl. Bartlett trying to help some of the others who were wounded and close by were three motionless bodies where Cpl.Bartlett had just finished firing his weapon. His determination and bravery had kept the Indonesians from coming any further. Lying close to me were two more who were obviously dead, judging by the amount of blood around them.

These Indonesians obviously hadn't realised that they were running into their own mortar fire because our 2 inch Mortars had been left behind in the ambush position and 2 Platoon had come out of the ambush with only their personal weapons. In the panic, they had left also behind their packs If they hadn't done so we might have suffered heavier casualties. By this time we knew that we had more wounded. Lt. Kirk had been shot and wounded and Pte Simpson, his arm severely mutilated, was being helped along by other platoon members. There was blood everywhere you turned. Cpl Bartlett and Lance Corporal Finn had been on their way out when they were wounded - Finn in the lower back and buttocks from mortar shrapnel and Bartlett in the neck. They were in great pain.

The Indonesians were still advancing towards us and everyone was in a blind panic, helping each other and screaming warnings over the sound of the gunfire.

Evacuation casualties from the border

Shrapnel was slamming into the trees, just missing our heads and burying metal into the ground. Hot metal was whizzing just millimetres away from our bodies and mortar shrapnel tugged at our clothes. It was like firing into nowhere - one minute you saw them and the next they had vanished into the trees. There was still a large amount of fire power coming towards us. Major Arnot was close by, kneeling at the side of a tree and firing short bursts whilst Lt Kirk, blood gushing from his leg was also doing his best to get us out of there. The gun battle was still going on as members of 3 Platoon took over the stretcher with Griffiths' body on it and helped with the wounded.

We called for air support and the courage of the response was amazing as the helicopter pilot hovered to evacuate the three most serious cases, Private Simpson, Lance Cpl Finn together with Lt. Kirk. As it took off from an improvised helipad, the rotor blades of the helicopter virtually touched the tops of the trees and on one occasion did so, breaking about four feet out of one blade. We all wondered if it was going to get out of there as it hovered for what seemed an age and all this while under enemy fire! The pilot was probably well aware that he would not be able to land again and it was a relief to see him fly off through a gap in the canopy of the trees into the open skies with a damaged rotor blade. The three soldiers that went out on the chopper would surely have died if they had not got out as their injuries were certainly life-threatening.

Mortars in action from a border base

Chapter 16

Carrying Griffiths' body / Enemy Mortar Fire / Geordie Reay Missing / '1 Platoon' goes as Search Party / Geordie Reay Found / Machine Gun in the Paddy Fields

As there was no time to get anybody else out, 3 Platoon had gone ahead of us to prepare a helipad and hacked the bush to the ground, but this had to be abandoned after that one airlift. Major Arnot had decided that it was unsafe to attempt another rescue by chopper and because Griffiths' body was not, of course, going to be left behind, we had no choice but to carry it and the three remaining wounded out. If another chopper had been called, it would certainly have been shot down as it hovered above us at three hundred feet, so we withdrew with great haste. Two aircraft from RAF Kuching had covered our initial drops of supplies and had made two or three runs over the enemy positions until Major Arnot got on the radio and instructed the howitzers at the base camp to take over and put down a barrage of artillery fire instead. We could hear him shouting the 'Alpha Company' call sign and giving the grid references of the enemy positions over the radio. We were still under heavy mortar fire and whilst we were withdrawing, we could see the Indonesians running towards us firing short bursts of gunfire and we continued returning it until they realised our artillery was pouring down on them. They didn't come any further then, but did manage to keep up the mortar fire for several hours. Our artillery were firing for a period of over two hours and we gradually realised that we were up against a much larger force than we had at first thought.

It dawned on us how lucky we had been. But for the map-reading abilities, skills and accuracy of Major Arnot, we would have suffered heavy losses and I don't know to this day how we would have managed to get out of there without his leadership. We had, by this time, released the two civilians in our custody and given them some rice from the emergency ration packs we had left and which we carried on our belts in our back pouches. We saw no point in keeping them with us, as they would only slow down our retreat. When we let them go, they ran like hell.

Barella, Noble, March and I were put on stretcher-party relief, relieving 3 Platoon. I took over from Dougy Elliot and I will never forget the look of fear on each man's face as we took the weight of Griffiths' body, which was wrapped in a ground sheet. We started our journey, back up the steep border, with our rifles slung over our shoulders and grabbing at tree branches with the free hands to pull ourselves up. The platoon commander was in front encouraging us to keep going, but it was a struggle. It was like climbing a wall - on one occasion we lost our footing whilst crossing a river when a shell - probably one of our own - exploded close by. The stretcher jerked out of our grasp and Griffiths' body fell away from us. I got back to my feet, but at that moment everyone had frozen into immobility as they looked at the body in the water lodged between two rocks. Alan Barella started shouting, "C'mon lads, pick 'im up! He winna hurt yeh man, he's deid now! Pick'm up an' let's get ta hell outa here!"

We picked Tom up and got a move on. As we did so, Major Arnot, who was close by, checked that every body who had been in the ambush position prior to action commencing was now present. We could hear him saying every man's name as he went through his personal little roll-call and as he moved amongst us he would say, "Well done, Geordie! Keep up the good work, it's not over yet!" As we rushed along the jungle track, we would hear one of our own shells explode behind us as though they were following us out of there. As the first two shells of our offensive fire had knocked out one of the Indonesian mortar sections, we had the comforting knowledge that our lads were certainly on target.

It was about 14.00hrs and though we could hear the enemy mortar shells exploding and the shrapnel whistling past us, it hit the trees and not us because they were landing short. On the odd occasion, we would hear short bursts of automatic fire and we got the impression that they were firing blindly into the jungle in panic. Our long struggle was nearly over. By the time we got to the top of the border, it was about 16.30hrs and with shells still exploding around us, we arrived at the helipad that we had cleared of mines and booby traps the previous week for the C.O's visit. No-one could then have foretold that it would be used for evacuating the dead and wounded from the action that had taken place earlier that day. We learned that up to now, about eighty artillery shells had been fired from our base camp.

We were all exhausted as we laid Griffiths' body at the corner of the helipad and two men were put on sentry duty as we got the radio into operation. That is when we were informed that all helicopters had been grounded until first light the following morning. By this time, Bali Ringin and the other two forward base camps, Nibong and Pluman Mapu were giving covering fire with their howitzers. Every couple of minutes we could hear the crack of the shell- fire in our support. All we could do was to disappear into the cover of the jungle and as we did so, we knew that we wouldn't be getting any sleep that night. It was to turn out to be the longest night we would ever experience in Borneo. It was pitch black, as the weather as changing rapidly and an electric storm rolled in, we could see lightening striking the tops of the trees as the rain lashed down.The monsoon season had started and as we couldn't see the man next to us, we had to resort to whispering to each other in an effort to maintain contact. We all thought the battle was over and that we would be making our way back to base camp at first light.

The platoon commander had a roll call and to our amazement, we were one man short - little Geordie Raey! He was a little fella, five-foot nowt, curly-haired and 'ard as nails.' Even though I was from Hartlepool, I couldn't understand his Geordie twang. We were told that he must be still in the ambush position and that someone must go back for him. At this time, we had no idea where he actually was, but certainly, that was the only place he could be. Just my luck, I was one of eight from '1 Section' to be included in the party who had to go on the search. We were led by the platoon commander and the rest of the party was made up of Lance Corporal Patterson, Pte. Kelly, Barella, Noble, Garroway, Miller, Thackeray and Lenny March. We carried only our personal weapons, a water bottle on our belts and a C41 radio that we would each take turns in carrying. The lads couldn't believe that we were going back to what we had just come out of - especially in the dark. It was pitch black and we did not know what to think, but we knew that we had to get Pte Reay back. We just hoped that the platoon commander knew what he was doing.

It was now about 19.30hrs and Major Arnot gave us a short briefing. 2 & 3 Platoons were to stay on the border with the remainder of 1 Platoon until we returned or needed any assistance. We started off down the border to the ambush position, carrying an 'M15 Armalite' and one 'Night Light' between us which was only to be used for map reading, to make sure we were on the right track. We kept so close together that we were virtually on top of each other in order to be sure that no-one wandered off in the wrong direction. All we could see were fire flies in front of us - thousands of them - and we prayed that we wouldn't get lost. By about 20.30hrs, it was still pitch black and it seemed a long time since we had left the border position. We don't usually move at night - it's just too dangerous - but we could not allow Pte Raey to fall into enemy hands.

By now we were on our way back down the Indonesian side of the border and couldn't see a fucking thing. We hoped that the platoon commander knew what he was doing and that he wasn't going to get us hopelessly astray - he stopped every ten or fifteen metres to check and recheck his compass bearing. Suddenly I fell and must have slid twenty feet straight into a running stream. All I heard then was "Come on Kelly! Get a fucking grip!" Well I was bloody soaking and had to feel about the ground to recover my rifle and struggle back to my feet. Some of the lads helped me up the embankment and I was right pissed off, but we carried on and were about a hundred metres from the position we had held when the ambush had been sprung when we heard gunfire. The enemy had heard us coming but if we couldn't see them, they couldn't see us either.

We were shouting, "RAEY…WHERE ARE YOU?" and this went on for half an hour. We didn't dare shine a light and in the pitch black were bumping into trees, sliding and falling, until we heard automatic gunfire, which seemed to be a short distance away. We advanced, crawling on all fours from tree to tree with our rifles cradled across both arms, until we could see the flashes from the muzzles of the weapons. We were still shouting, "REAY…WHERE ARE YOU ?" when suddenly we heard him. "SIR…I'M OVER HERE!" the platoon commander said, "What are you doing here?" and he replied, "Wye sur…yeh put mi 'ere yes'day gerdin' an' told mi ta stey 'ere an' 'old this position, en' neebody come back so 'ere ah am sur!" - all of this in broad Geordie.

He was shaking, either from fear or from the cold. The Indonesians knew he was there but somehow he had managed to hold them off all day, using almost all of his ammunition for the Bren gun. Out of four magazines and a bandolier of two hundred rounds, he had half a magazine left. This explained the automatic fire we had heard on our way up. At that moment, a flare rose into the sky, lighting the jungle so we all lay very still. We realised how he had managed to survive. He was on higher ground so it would have been suicide for the Indonesians to try to over-run him, and they didn't know he was on his own.

It was time for us all to get out of there. We put Reay in front so that he would be first out and two of us remained three or four metres behind to give covering fire in case they tried to follow us. As we were on our way up the border, we were about half-way back, being very careful and alert, when at that moment we heard a kind of 'pop' sound and Noble shouted, "MORTAR FIRE!" and we all curled up like balls behind trees. We heard them explode to the right of us and decided to keep going. All the way back up to the border, the mortar fire continued landing some hundred metres short of our positions. We had done this patrol twice in less than twelve hours - but this time we practically carried each other to make sure that no-one was left behind. Our names were being called by the platoon commander every five or ten minutes. We were so closely bunched together that we were literally holding on to each other. If we hadn't, we knew that we would surely have lost somebody in the total darkness.

As I was the last man, I was going to make damn sure that I for one wasn't going to be left behind. When we arrived at the top of the border, where the rest of the platoon were waiting, we got in touch over the radio and told them that we were about to come in and as we entered, one by one, we would give our name and last two 'Service numbers'. At night and with all the camouflage cream, you would be very difficult to recognise. You would hear, "ADVANCE AND BE RECOGNISED!" and in we went one by one. I was the last man and I remember Sgt. Charlton saying, "Where's that black-headed fucker Kelly?" I remember removing my bush hat to wipe my forehead and he shuffled my hair and said, "Well done!"

It was just before first light when we arrived. The platoon commander had certainly lived up to his reputation for map reading. We rested for about thirty minutes before starting on our journey back to the base camp and, as daylight came very quickly, we set off, knowing that it would take about five or six hours.

We could hear the sound of the helicopter circling above us and preparing to land. As it did so, we ran towards it with the stretcher carrying Griffiths' body between us. We loaded it and the wounded as fast as we could and suddenly it was airborne again and flying off into the distance.

We pulled out to start our descent back down the Sarawak side of the border, carrying all our equipment and back packs which we had recovered from the RV together with some of 2 Platoon's equipment belonging to the wounded and an extra two Bren guns which we passed around to share the load. When we arrived at the bottom of the border, 3 Platoon and the remainder of 2 Platoon had left shortly before on the journey back to base camp, so they were well in front of us. Time seemed to pass so quickly that we were back on level ground and patrolling the jungle track before we realised it. It was about ten o'clock in the morning when we were told to stop because we were approaching two rice paddy fields. We could see the 'string bridges', as we called them, which were made out of bamboo and twine to make handrails to hold on to. They spanned the swamp-like fields to our front and as we came out of the jungle to a clearing, suddenly there were bullets flying everywhere as a machine gun post opened up at the far end of the field.

We immediately melted back into the relative safety of the jungle. If they had waited just a few more minutes, we would have suffered heavy casualties. Luckily for us, the machine gunner must have had itchy fingers. The platoon commander got on the radio almost immediately to ask for artillery fire and within minutes, the shells started raining down. They soon found their target after the platoon commander corrected the enemies' grid reference and twenty rounds from the howitzers from Gunin Gadja fell right on target. Not taking any chances, we went around the paddy field until we found the machine gun, or what was left of it, and craters everywhere the shells had landed. We found no trace of life. Mind you, after that bombardment, there would not be much left of them anyway if they had remained at their post - either that or they had run off into the jungle. They wouldn't have stood a chance.

We were, at last, back on the 'A1' track towards our base, being very careful and alert and walking six metres apart. All we needed now was to walk into an enemy ambush! It took almost another four hours to get back to the river at the bottom of the camp, which everybody was pleased to see. Then we had the five hundred and thirty nine steps to crack. When we reached the top of Guning Gadja, I remember the men taking their packs off and seeing the backs of their shirts all wringing wet and soaked with sweat.

I walked in last with a Bren gun at my waist and the strap around my neck. Everybody was exhausted. We were greeted by Lt. Col. Maughan, the C/O of the battalion and all the lads were applauding and cheering. We all received a half a cup of rum.

Going on R & R to Kuching

Chapter 17

Back at 'Guning Gadja' / Clean-up and Debriefing / Singing Party in the NAAFI / Bali Ringin and 'RR' in Kuching / Death of Miller / Back at Bali Ringin / More Action at Pluman Mapu

They were all pleased to see us back and all the rest of the company were asking us what had happened. All we wanted was a shower and a rest because we hadn't washed or shaved for three or four days. So we cleaned up and had a few hours sleep and afterwards we were told to report to the NAAFI for a debriefing on the ambush. We told of our individual parts in the ambush and of the casualties we had suffered - one dead and five wounded, which included the platoon commander. We had killed twenty seven of the enemy and wounded several, it was confirmed when the engagement came to an end. The SAS reported that our artillery had killed twenty six Indonesian troops in the village of Lubok Sabot in the bombardment. The damaged helicopter was being fitted with a new blade and we thought how lucky they had been after having had to make an emergency landing at the base and transferring the wounded to another chopper.

The company commander told us the good news that we were about to go on 'RR' (Rest and Recuperation) for a week in Kuching, and that was the end of that. He told us that the NAAFI was now open and that the first two cans were on him. After we had downed the two 'extra' from the C/O, we had our 'normal' allowance of two cans.

We were in a hut which was built with bamboo and had a tin roof that we used as a NAAFI. When it was coming in dark, we could close down some flaps on the windows and light candles. Then the singing started and we had a few more cans as the Colour Sergeant Bob Fawcett, was very generous that night and we were all half cut. He said that we were allowed more on this occasion because a Welsh platoon was doing all the guard duties for the next 24 hours. We had a great party with Barella starting the singing, and he was very good. Next was Miller with his banjo, singing 'On Mother Kelly's Doorstep'. It was one good night, because we were so pleased that our 'tribulations' were over, for the time being.

Because two days later we would be heading for Kuching, we spent the next two days cleaning weapons, getting all our kit back up to scratch and reporting any lost equipment. We had lost a Bren gun and the two spare barrels we had carried together with two 2 inch Mortars plus a lot of personal packs and rations. This was the Colour Sergeant's problem now - we couldn't give a fuck and everybody was having a laugh and a joke about it. All this had to be completed by 14.00hrs by which time we would have to report to the helipad in clean, pressed OG's. When the helicopters started arriving, our platoon was waiting with each man on his knees, having a webbing belt with two magazines and one hand holding a rifle whilst trying to hold his bush hat on with the other. As they landed, we were running towards them in sticks of eight and their rotor blades were still turning over our heads as we boarded, so that they could get a quick take off.

As we arrived in Bali Ringin, the RSM took control and ordered us to fall in. He had to have his little inspection before we left and a scream at us to let us know that he was still the boss. We had just come out of the biggest gun battle the battalion had ever had in Borneo and he couldn't give a fuck...he still treated us exactly the same, like dogs!

We helped unload the cargo of stores and ammunition for the howitzers and mortars from the Bedford RLs in we were to travel to Kuching. As we climbed into the open -backed lorries, we carried our personal 7.62 SLR weapons and there was also a GPMG mounted on the tailboard. Two 'Saracen Scout Cars' were positioned at either end of the convoy and we were on high alert because when travelling in open trucks, there was always a risk of getting ambushed. It was a very dusty journey and as we travelled at high speed along the Kuching road, Miller, Barella, Noble and myself were sitting on the rear end of the trucks, holding on to ropes and the backs of the seats. It was some bumpy ride and we were pleased to see the end of the journey.

There to meet us was Colour Sergeant Durham accompanied by two Military Policemen ('Redcaps' as they were known). We were marched to a Nissen hut and the 'Redcap' sergeant gave us a speech on what was out of bounds and what wasn't. Any drunken brawls in bars and we would be arrested and returned to our unit. We handed our weapons in to the stores and were told that our accommodation had been arranged at the Palm Grove Hotel. That was when the colour sergeant warned us about the local women and the diseases they carried. If we went with them it would be at our own risk. He said that one third of the last platoon had caught VD or other diseases. I had heard enough. That put me off straightaway. I would stick to the drink. As we entered the hotel, young women stood at the doorway trying to pick us up because they knew we had money. We were allowed two hundred Malayan dollars each and we were all bent on having a good time visiting all the bars and nightclubs.

The hotel, which was an eight-storey building, was all paid for by the army and we were all on the very top floor. We would be up till three in the morning, sometimes later. We had keys to our rooms but half the lads went straight into the bar next door with some of the women and stayed there until they were legless. Garroway (whom I nicknamed "Gatt") and I went to a market to get some civilian clothes because we just couldn't wait to get out of the 'Jungle Greens' we were wearing. All the clothes we needed were a thin shirt and some slacks in this hot climate. Then we returned to the hotel to find the party in the next-door bar was still going on.

There were the lads, with three or four women around them, spending money as if there were to be no tomorrow and asking us to buy some drinks as we walked in. I told them not to be daft and asked them if they thought I was a nutcase altogether? If we started doing things like that our money would be gone in no time at all and we still had another four days left. I didn't fancy spending the rest of my 'RR' in my hotel room. I found there was a card game going on - 'Three Card Brag' and there as a large pot in the middle of the table which meant that somebody was losing their leave pay and that there would be a few of them skint on the first day - probably asking us to lend them money. No chance!

Miller, Noble and Barella were sitting at the table, so we joined their company, drinking rum and cokes. Miller was saying that if he had been in Hong Kong, he would have gone 'AWOL' (Absent Without Leave) because he didn't want to go back to the jungle. We really thought he meant it and a lot of the lads felt the same way, but we had to go back. I was talking to Miller most of the time and realised what a really nice bloke he was, though he looked like a right hard case.

It was getting late and I was absolutely shattered, because I couldn't take the hard drink. I managed to crawl up the stairs and get into bed. and I knew that I would have a big headache in the morning.

The next few days we spent drinking and visiting bars with women and all-night parties. I didn't like to admit that I hadn't had a lot to do with women, but I had met a nice dark-haired girl in one of the many bars and she didn't take much persuading to come back to the hotel with me to have a drink. As we walked into the hotel, all the lads took the piss, shouting, "Kelly's scored!" She didn't speak a word of English but with the lads trying to get me drunk, it wasn't hard to believe that I would. I remember going up to my room with her and waking up about two in the morning to find she was gone - probably to join a party that was going on, or maybe one of the lads had come in and taken her.

I came to my senses very quickly and checked my pockets to see if my money was still there. It was. Afterwards, I couldn't remember or even care what she looked like. The first girl I had ever had anything to do with and she was of oriental origin. It was all over in two or three hours and I was worried in case I had caught anything. By this time, she was probably being shared out amongst the lads and having a good time, in fact I had probably been her invitation to the party.

On R & R in Kuching
Left-right: myself, Bob Noble, Charlie Bassett and unknown from A Company Stores

Listening to the brawling that was going on, we didn't get much sleep what with Miller singing all night and the clashing of the crates of Tiger beer being dragged up the stairs and the women, one after the other, shrieking with laughter.

I decided to rejoin the party, since I couldn't sleep - it must have been around 2.30 in the morning. It was all going on in this large room with four single beds. Barella, Noble and Donaldson were on the floor drinking with a few females and all the lads were singing. Miller was sitting on a window ledge playing his mouth-organ and with the ceiling fan spinning to cool the room down, we were all having a great time, until Miller disappeared from the window ledge and the window doors began banging against the outside wall. Then everybody realised that Miller had fallen from the seventh floor and everybody looked at each other in disbelief.

As total shock took over, we all sobered up immediately. Allen and Nobby ran for the door and made their way down the stairs. As we got to the street at the front of the hotel, a crowd was already gathering and when we got to Miller, we could see that he was in a bad way. When the military police arrived immediately afterwards, the news was broken that Miller was dead because of a tragic accident. We were questioned for the rest of that night as the investigation to establish the cause of his death proceeded. We were all in shock, we sat in the hotel bar all morning in total silence. Durnall was upset and crying uncontrollably - he being another eighteen year old sent out at the same time as I had been. Having been at Miller's side since we arrived, they had become great friends.

It was the last two days in Kuching and the good times had come to an end. We hadn't the heart to go anywhere and as the army were not going to alter their plans no matter what had happened, we had another two days to sit out. I was looking forward to buying a Seiko watch which was worth about three hundred pounds in England and could be bought here for about ten dollars. I was not going home empty-handed while I still had some money left. I got up early with 'Gatt' to head down to the market and I managed to find a watch for twelve dollars - a real bargain. After a few drinks and some sight-seeing, we made our way back to the hotel to find the police still swarming all over the place and some of the lads all sitting talking quietly about Miller and having a drink.

Having had such a good time the night before with our friend Geordie Miller so happy, laughing and playing his mouth organ or banjo, we found that it was now turning into a total nightmare and we were in shock. It was such a short time since I had helped to carry the body of my best friend's brother up the Indonesian border for about seven miles. Because Griffiths' death had happened so recently, some of the lads were still in Singapore after his funeral and I wondered to myself when was this going to end? Darnell had been closest to Geordie Miller who had looked after him like a little brother.

Bob Griffith was sent back to England on compassionate grounds and would not be returning to Borneo. Some of the lads were selected to go to Miller's funeral. There was no explanation possible for his death and he was buried in Singapore with full military honours a few days after Griffiths, who was buried on the 2nd of March 1966. They lie in the Ulu Pandan cemetery in Singapore.

Now the 'RR' was in ruins, nobody wanted to stay in Kuching after what had happened. It was soon time to board the Bedford RLs for our return trip to Bali Ringing and the front line base camps. As we entered the camp, we could see the RAF ground crews refuelling the Belvederes and Wessex helicopters. The GPMGs were being tested with short bursts of fire into the pepperfields and RSM Ford was there to greet us as usual. He was the Helicopter Tasking Officer at Bali Ringin and the minute we were inside the camp we were told to fall in. He bellowed in a loud voice, "After your little trip, I'm sure you must all be a little stiff! So while waiting for the CO, we will loosen up!" and he marched us around the helipad at the same blistering hundred and eighty paces to the minute, breaking then into double time. It was no fun after drinking all week and some of the lads were ill. The hot sun didn't help and the flying beetles and mosquitoes all had a go at us. It simply wasn't at all funny and we were praying for the CO to show up so that we could relax.

At last we were stood easy and the CO started his briefing. He told us to put behind us all that had happened over the past three weeks and that there was rioting going in Jakarta. There were two squadrons of Special Air Service troops from Australia on standby along the border plus several artillery batteries and the Royal Australian Navy and elements of the British fleet including H.M.S. Bulwark were in the surrounding waters. Up to that date, twenty-three Australians had been killed in the fighting. He was trying to tell us that the risk of enemy contact was greater than ever before and that, when we returned to the forward base, we must be on full alert.

When the C/O's briefing was over, the Wessex 'Whirlwinds' were landing on the helipad for us to board. After the flight, we were told that the helicopter would hover about three feet from the ground and then we would have to jump. Once we were out, the chopper would fly straight off.

It was a strange feeling to be back to the barbed wire and sandbagged trenches with the muzzles of the machine guns pointing outwards from the bunkers towards the jungle. It was strangely reassuring to find the rats and snakes still there, chasing each other round our living quarters and making themselves at home. The looks on the lads' faces would be difficult to interpret. We were going to be the first platoon out later that week, just getting back into the routine of border patrols. Whilst we had been on leave, we had had some new arrivals and they were Kiwis. We were ordered to take eight men from the Royal New Zealand Light Infantry on patrol with us. This was the battalion that was to relieve us in coming months. They were dark, tanned, built like a rugby team and very friendly.

These soldiers were used to the jungle, and though they were late in coming into this war against Sukarno, they had been serving alongside other British troops in Borneo who had lost more than twenty men and had many wounded. At this point there was a force of at least twelve thousand troops in Borneo, of which more than half were British: '2 Para' and Marine Commandos, two companies of Special Air Services and, of course, the Ghurkas. Indonesian casualties were put at over 600 killed as a result of our cross-border operations.

It was time for our first patrol since returning from Kuching and it would take us to 'C' Company's position, called Nibong. This was another well-protected camp, dug into the hillside with a connecting trench system, bunkers and a command centre similar to our own. It was strange to be on this patrol with two of my mates missing, Miller being dead and Bob Griffiths having been sent home on compassionate grounds after Tommy's funeral in Singapore. I simply had to get along without them and as a result made even closer friendships with Barella and Noble who were both good lads and built like Sonny Liston.

When we had spent a day at Nibong and got a good meal down us, thanks to 'C' Company, we left at first light next morning for Pluman Mapu, where 'B'

Company were positioned. We had information that a small force of Indonesians were close by and that our position was likely to come under enemy attack - not for the first time, as it had been assailed in force by Indonesian border troops in a previous engagement. At this time, the 2nd Battalion, the Parachute Regiment were occupying the camp which was commanded by Captain John Flemming, together with Captain Webb who was in control of a 105mm Howitzer and a mortar section. In the same company was a Sgt. Major Williams who was decorated for bravery at a later date after he was wounded and lost an eye. It made me feel pretty good to hear these stories, because this was the battalion I was going to join on my return to England, if I passed 'P' Company. I was determined to pass, even though everyone thought I was a lunatic, because every chance I got, I was doing press-ups and running. I took all the advice that Jack Connor, the ex-Para had given me when I was in training.

Alan Barella, Billy Forman and Tony Barella in the NAAFI

Chapter 18

Pluman Mapu / Enemy Attack / 'Hearts & Minds' / Komodo Dragon! / I collapse on Patrol / Bali Ringin & 'Florrie' Ford / Time to Return to the UK

When we arrived at Pluman Mapu, 'B Company' welcomed us. Again, it was like going up the 'five hundred and thirty nine steps', similar to our own camp and we had a lot of remarks - which I won't repeat - from the lads about never, ever visiting 'B' Company again. Just as we settled in, the first Indonesian shell landed with a huge bang, luckily between the perimeter fence and the camp. As we all jumped for cover, we could hear our GPMGs opening up immediately on all the guard posts. The mortar section also went into action and all we could do was stay under cover, avoid the shrapnel and wait for things to calm down.

We knew, by now, how the Indonesians worked. It was 'hit and run' but this went on for another two hours. It was clear that they were trying to over-run the camp and the only way to stop this new attack was by a heavy amount of fire-power. We were told to go below ground and man the bunkers because all of these had holes facing outwards towards to perimeter fence and you could point a Bren gun and sweep over a 45 degree angle, firing continuously. Because the 32 rounds in a magazine didn't last long, the 'No.2' had to be quick in filling the empty magazines. As for myself, I was issued with an American 'M15 Armalite' which was probably because I had been carrying an 'A41' radio set and which was taken from me by the signals operator when the attack started.

By this time the Indonesians were on the run, but to their surprise the SAS were operating in our area, close to the border and had something in store for them. An ambush had been planned for them as they made their way back to the border and the Indonesians suffered heavy losses during that day.

I got talking to the lads - one of whom, in particular, I already knew as I had seen him before: a Pte Joe Gahan who had a London accent. Then we realised that he had lived in Kendal Road in Hartlepool - just a couple of hundred yards from where I lived, where he had moved when he was fourteen. The lads were 'taking the Mick' and saying that when we got back to England, they were going to enrol

A patrol leaving Gunin Gadja camp

Joe in Gateshead University to teach him the Geordie language. We were to become great friends after Borneo.

Next morning, we planned to return to Kampong Bunan Gega (nicknamed 'Gunning Gadja') and we left 'B' Company to clean up the mess and to practically rebuild some of the gun positions. On the way back, some of the lads were chatting amongst themselves and wondering what might happen if there was an attack on our camp before we got back, as it was well under strength. It was slow progress getting through the jungle and we were lucky to make seven hundred metres a day as we chopped our way through the thick undergrowth whilst keeping a watch up on the 100ft high trees. We weren't looking for orang-outangs, but enemy ambushes. If they remained perfectly still either on the ground or up in the trees, it would be impossible to see them until you were almost on top of them, but by then it would be too late. That is why you always had to have your wits about you and keep a watchful eye both on the treetops and on the ground for booby traps and punjee sticks. One member of our platoon had a bad experience with one of the latter. It ripped along the side of his jungle boot and split it from top to bottom - luckily without marking his leg. Again luckily for him, one of the lads had a spare set of boots in his pack just about his size. As we approached our camp, we were told to carry out a perimeter patrol at the camp which had 'stood to' the previous night because someone had reported noises and opened up with a machine gun. After what had happened to 'B' Company everybody was jumpy.

Because we had been lumbered with this task, it took about two hours to get around the perimeter, and it was hard work. We were walking around the side of a steep hill, about a third of the way up, and it was very difficult to keep your footing and chop your way through the thick undergrowth. We eventually got around to the main entrance only to find that the place was deserted - everybody had gone, though there were signs that someone had been there.

Everyone was pleased to be back if only to get out of the clothes we had worn for the last five days and get cleaned up. Our weapons needed a good clean and we attended to this, one section at a time, as a precaution in case we were attacked and were caught off guard. The clothes we had been wearing were thrown into a heap, ready for the 'Dhobi' man.

We had a lazy few days lying out in the sun interspersed with a couple of hours in the NAAFI. It was so different without Miller and Griffiths and everyone was conscious of it. We did get some stories and laughs out of our New Zealand friends who had arrived as an advance party. I remember one of them had a chameleon lizard on a piece of cotton thread and he was trying to train it. What a nutter! Everywhere he placed the lizard, it changed colour and he got so excited that he was still moving it around the next day.

We were told we were getting a visitor. It was Padre Harris and he gathered us all on the helipad for a service for Griffiths and Miller and there were a few tears that day when he called the names of the dead and wounded, because it was all still in the back of our minds. When it was all over, it was back to normal and we spent the rest of the day cleaning the Bren guns and the gimpies.

Three days had passed in camp and one section of the platoon was sent to Kampong, just outside the camp, at the bottom of the hill on a 'Hearts and Minds' operation. To get to this, we had to cross the river, up to waist height in the water, to treat some of the occupants - mainly children - who had some sort of infection. We were the escort for the M.O. who was to treat these people and some of the sights we saw were unbelievable. Some women had clothes wrapped around their waists. Their breasts were non-existent because they were literally rotting away with some sort of disease (leprosy) and it was a horrifying sight to see. The male population didn't look too clever either, but all we could do was try to give them some sort of comfort such as some chocolate and biscuits from our rations. The M.O. would be dishing out the codeine tablets!. That's all we could do and then it was time to make the climb back up to the camp. The sights I saw in this kampong made me wonder how people managed to exist in these jungles, but somehow they did.

Our tour was coming to an end. We had only two patrols left to do before going home to Colchester and we were looking forward to it.We were preparing to leave 'Gunan Gadja' but this time we were accompanied by the Ghurkas, the Kiwis and the SAS. All together there was a force of thirty-six men - well over platoon strength. This was one patrol I wouldn't forget.

It was the first day of the patrol and I saw myself as one of the fittest men in the platoon. We had covered a lot of ground and we were travelling faster than ever before for some reason unknown to us. We made camp that night without any incident and the following day we came to a river which we didn't cross but went up it instead, all the time at waist height. On both sides all you could see was rocks and cliffs with the river running towards you and we must have seen every creature in the jungle. As we came out of the water and onto dry land, we said, "Thank fuck for that!" and then started clearing an area to make camp.

What I then saw in front of me was a fucking great crocodile-like thing. It turned out to be a rare species of reptile called a Komodo dragon, and it was about twelve feet long. I thought I was seeing things as it opened its mouth and started shooting its long tongue towards me. I was terrified, but a couple of the lads attacked it with their machetes to stop it attacking me. When they hacked into it, it began spinning everywhere, then it was dead. I think now that we should have tried to get it back into the river as I don't think it really meant me any harm and it was probably more scared than we were, but it was too late and the damage was done. We made camp and thought that it was unlikely that we would be attacked that night as it was the thickest jungle we had come across and everyone was exhausted, though we stayed on the alert at all times.

Next day, we were climbing up to the border and because it didn't rain for some reason, it was so hot that the shirt and trousers were sticking to me and every so often you would have to pull your shirt from where it was sticking to your body underneath your webbing and pack. At times we were down to our knees as we were pushed really hard. Barella could see how I was struggling so he took the radio from me and told me to keep going. That was comradeship for you. Because I was struggling and the lads could see it, I felt really ashamed of myself. I was slowing them down - and after my telling them that I was going to join the Parachute Regiment! I didn't think it would get to me but it did. Next morning I awoke to find that Barella and Noble had covered my guard duty during the night. These men were real heroes and good friends.

Before we started again up the border, I didn't feel like eating any chocolate or biscuits and from the first few steps I knew there was something wrong. I felt like shit and after an hour of struggling and crawling and grabbing at tree branches I started to shake and all my body was quivering, and then I collapsed. It was as if I was having a fit.

I can remember all of them gathering around me. I couldn't go on any longer and they knew it. The Kiwi soldiers put me up against a tree and one of the SAS men was trying to dry the sweat off me. He then removed my shirt and got some dry

Signals Observation post on the border

clothes on me, telling me to take salt tablets. He started talking to me saying, "The lads told me that you intend joining the Parachute Regiment on your return to England." He told me not to let this little incident put me off and that he had been in 1 Para before joining the SAS. I never found out his name and have never seen him since.

We were not very far from the top of the border and they knew that they would have to carry me. The soldier who was giving me the tablets told me not to worry and added, "This happens to the best of us in this climate and terrain. It could be a touch of malaria." Since we were almost on the edge of the equator, it was very hot and humid. They made a stretcher out of an Australian lightweight poncho and, since the jungle was too thick to make a helipad, they intended to carry me and my kit to an easier place to get me out. The only way out was up and I didn't want to inflict this terrific labour on them and tried to tell them so, but they wouldn't listen. I had no choice in the matter. They struggled for the rest of that day and it was early evening when they decided to make camp.

Pte Garroway made a bivouac to conceal the light while he made a brew-up and a meal for himself and me out of some hard-tack biscuits, a meat block and some curry powder. When it was dark, everything fell silent and it felt as if you were on your own, it was so quiet. There were only ants that you would be pulling off your bodies and the fireflies whose aerial manoeuvres we watched. There were millions of them and they presented such an amazing sight that before you knew it, it would be first light that meant 'stand to your positions'. As usual you would hear the shells from the howitzers at our base camps and we stood down.

I was told that there was a helicopter coming in shortly to pick me up, but I didn't realise that we were only a short distance from the helipad that our platoon had cleared of mines on a previous patrol, when we had the contact with the Indonesians a few weeks before. It was about 07.30hrs when I heard the sound of the chopper coming in and one of the lads ran out onto the helipad as soon as it was ascertained that it was one of ours.

I was carried to the side of the 'Sioux' helicopter. This glass-fronted machine was designed to take two men of average weight and I was strapped into a box that was attached to the side. All I could see was the glass front of the chopper and it took off immediately. The journey took about 25 minutes and when it landed it was obvious that it was Bali Ringing. Then I heard a loud voice and I thought to myself, "Oh no!" A face looked in at me and nearly frightened me to death. It was 'Florrie Ford' - another nickname we had given him was 'A Quarter to Three' because his toes and heels were in perfect straight line when he stood to attention. All I heard was, "KELLY-GET-OUT-OF-THERE!" and that was above the noise of the helicopter. engines roaring. He put the fear of God into me. There I was, just wishing that I was with my friends on the border patrol. Before take-off I felt I was dying. During the flight I was semi-conscious, but the very second I heard 'Florrie's booming 'God-like' voice, I was up and running towards the Medical Centre. I was under the M.O. for 24hrs and then it was back to normal duties.

When I had calmed down and was talking to the M.O., he told me that Borneo was a strange place and that the climate could easily effect the fittest of us. He was probably trying to make me feel better. Right at that minute, I was feeling embarrassed and felt that I had let my mates down. He also said that it could have been a touch of malaria as well as heat exhaustion. I was told to stay in Bali Ringin for a week before returning to 'Gunnan Gadja'.

I was to meet up with Cpl. Norton again and he was to teach me mine warfare and booby-traps. It turned out to be very interesting. We started the first day reinforcing the perimeter fence and checking the claymores and trip-wires. This is when I met up again with Brian Constable, only this time as a free man. He was a member of the 'Assault Pioneer Platoon' together with Chris Higham, another Hartlepool lad. As we were doing some repairs to the perimeter fence, he would be following up behind us. They looked like a couple of divers, each with a bottle strapped to his back and with a pipe attached to a spray gun for killing such weeds and undergrowth as were left, to make the camp look more like a postcard - probably on instructions from the RSM.

Cpl. Norton was a very good instructor and I remember one occasion on the helipad he had this thing that looked like a thunder flash. It turned out to be an

Anti-Personnel Mine No. 8 which weighs about 8 ounces and is about 8 inches long. It is capable of blowing a man's legs off. Also on display were all sorts of 'Pull, Pressure & Release' switches and an anti-tank mine. At this stage I had found another point of interest in my army career. He taught me a lot in that week and I took it all in. He even asked me to transfer into his platoon on our return to Colchester and I was quite interested. Then it was time for me to return to 'Gunning Gadja'.

A 'Wessex' helicopter was coming in from Kuching with the mail for the lads in the forward base camps, and I was to board it. As it came in, I was kneeling on the helipad with all my kit, rifle and webbing and with the RSM alongside. We ran to the chopper and he took the postbag and made sure I was on board. As I climbed in, he shouted, "I DO NOT WANT TO SEE YOU HERE AGAIN! DO YOU HEAR ME KELLY?" and I screamed back, "YES SIR!"

The flight took about twenty minutes to base and, looking out of the doorway at the jungle beneath us was an amazing sight. I could see the mountain range where we had struggled on our patrols, so many times. Before we actually landed, I jumped to the ground with my head down and ran towards the camp with a rifle in one hand and the post in the other. As it turned out, the lads were pleased to see me and I was pleased to see my mates. I thought they would have 'taken the Micky' but they didn't.

I couldn't wait to get back into the routine of the patrols again. That night, Barella, my friends and I sat around the bunker waiting for a broadcast on Radio Malaysia and it was announced that a peace deal had been agreed in Bangkok. We were relieved and happy, but this was to make no difference to our way of life because the Indonesians continued to make incursions across the frontier and the threat to security was a real one. Although we didn't have another contact, our patrols found enemy activity which called for constant redeployment by helicopters and long, arduous patrolling with little to show for it, except the knowledge that we were achieving our aim of preventing the enemy from penetrating our battalion area. This went on for another two months until it was time to return to the UK.

Our move was complicated, as it meant that we had to travel by four different means: helicopter, road transport, three troop ships and fixed-wing aircraft. The companies moved out tactically from the base camps, leaving behind the Royal New Zealand Light Infantry who took over our camps and duties in Sarawak.

We arrived in Kuching to find three troop ships waiting for us. I boarded the troop ship MV. Auby, which was the same scrapper I had come across in. I was surprised to see that it was still afloat. The captain was another 'Geordie' and he held a cocktail party for the high-ups, officers and NCOs. A couple of us real soldiers were employed as waiters, dressed in our best, brand new 'OGs'. During this 'major military exercise', we were informed that Brigadier Cheyne was guest of honour together with the '99 Ghurka Brigade' staff and other dignitaries from Chungking. We didn't sail for thirty-six hours after. That's when the Tiger beer came out - crates of it. We were to spend another three or four days crossing the South China Sea.

Of course, the card games started below decks and the main offender was 'B' Company. I did get involved with one game of 'Brag' and it was my lucky day! I won so much money that I couldn't get it all in my kitbag. We arrived in Singapore harbour only to find Her Majesty's Customs waiting for us. They picked out one in ten and I was one of the unlucky ones.They took it all, less fifty Malaysian dollars, because I couldn't explain where I got it all from.

Here I was, where it had all started six months previously, in Nee Soon camp. Pretty soon we were boarding the aircraft for the long flight that was to take us back to England. I didn't think either the lads or myself would want to come within a thousand miles of Borneo again. We just couldn't wait to get home and when we got to Meanee Barracks, Colchester, we were to be sent on 112 days leave, though not before signing the Official Secrets Act. We were not allowed to tell anyone about operations in Borneo. I didn't even tell my mother and father. All they had had was our BFPO (British Forces Field Post Office) number and my father always thought that I had been in the Middle East because there was never anything in the British press. The secrecy went on for years to come and that is why we called it 'The Forgotten War'. On returning to the UK, after receiving my Borneo Medal with Clasp on a parade that HRH. Princess Alexandra attended, Major Arnot received the Military Cross and Corporal Bartlett was 'Mentioned in Despatches' as were Lieutenant Kirk together with RSM Ford.

In the months to come, we were sent on a tour to Malta and Denmark, then on to Cyprus for a six month tour with a United Nations Force. On returning to the UK, I was selected with other members of 'A' Company to take part in the Honour Guard on the Tyne Tunnel, which was opened by Her Majesty Queen Elizabeth II. It was a great honour for me. This turned out to be my last duty with the 1st Battalion the Durham Light Infantry. In the summer of 1967, my Para course came up and I went to Browning Barracks, Aldershot to do the 'P' Company and gained a 'Pass Plus'.

I then went on to the Support Company Anti Tank Platoon, the Parachute Regiment for the rest of my army career, but that's another story.

Geordie Miller's funeral in Singapore

INDEX

INDEX

INDEX

INDEX